GAUGUIN

MAKER OF MYTH

Edited by
Belinda Thomson

Consultant Editor
Tamar Garb

With contributions by
Philippe Dagen
Amy Dickson
Charles Forsdick
Tamar Garb
Vincent Gille
Linda Goddard
Belinda Thomson

Tate Publishing

National Gallery of Art, Washington

GAUGUIN

MAKER OF MYTH

Global exhibition sponsor
Bank of America Merrill Lynch

With additional support in London from The Gauguin Exhibition Supporters Group
The Annenberg Foundation
John and Susan Burns
Eykyn Maclean
Fares and Tania Fares
Patrick and Sophie Fauchier
Mark and Sophie Lewisohn
Catherine and Franck Petitgas
The Search Foundation
and those donors who wish to remain anonymous

First published 2010 by order of the Tate Trustees
by Tate Publishing, a division of Tate Enterprises Ltd,
Millbank, London SW1P 4RG
www.tate.org.uk/publishing

on the occasion of the exhibition
Gauguin: Maker of Myth
organised by Tate Modern, London, in association
with the National Gallery of Art, Washington

Tate Modern, London
30 September 2010 – 16 January 2011

National Gallery of Art, Washington
27 February – 5 June 2011

British Library Cataloguing in Publication Data
A catalogue record for this book is available from the British Library

ISBN
978 1 85437 982 5 (paperback)

Design concept by Why Not Associates
Layout by Miguel Rodrigues
Printed in Great Britain by St Ives Westerham Press

Cover: Paul Gauguin, *Manao tupapau* (detail), 1892, oil on burlap mounted on canvas,
Albright-Knox Art Gallery, Buffalo, A. Conger Goodyear Collection, 1965

Measurements of artworks are given in centimetres, height before width and depth

CONTENTS

SPONSOR'S FOREWORD

Brian Moynihan
President and Chief Executive Officer
Bank of America

Continuing our long tradition of support for the arts, Bank of America is pleased to present *Gauguin: Maker of Myth* in both London and Washington, DC. We look forward to creating common cultural experiences among museum-goers in different parts of the world; to working once again with two leading arts institutions, Tate Modern in London and the National Gallery of Art in Washington, DC; and to being part of one of the most comprehensive views of Gauguin's work in recent years.

　　More than 150 works ranging from sculptures to paintings to ceramics from arts institutions and private collectors around the world comprise this important exhibition, showing how the arts can bring people together around a shared interest. As our company becomes ever more global, with associates representing Bank of America, Bank of America Merrill Lynch, Merrill Lynch Wealth Management, MBNA and US Trust doing business in more than 100 countries, we know that greater cultural understanding leads to greater economic opportunity.

　　We hope you enjoy *Gauguin: Maker of Myth* and are able to share this special experience with family and friends. We also hope that you, like us, will value the opportunity to share a rich cultural experience with hundreds of thousands of people from around the globe.

FOREWORD

Nicholas Serota
Director, Tate

Earl A. Powell III
Director, National Gallery of Art

Paul Gauguin (1848–1903) is one of the most influential and celebrated artists of the nineteenth century. His paintings work powerfully at a formal level, their intensity of colour and synthetic use of line making an immediate impact. Their enigmatic and allusive content, too, continues to hold a fascination, added to which it is an inescapable fact that Gauguin's colourful life looms as large as his art in the public imagination. The purpose of Gauguin: Maker of Myth is to present this complex and challenging artist to a twenty-first-century audience in a fresh and compelling way. Gauguin's play with poetic narrative, myth and fable – judged somewhat reactionary in the context of modernism – has a long legacy in the twentieth century; it is arguably a strategy that speaks today to artists and audiences who have moved a long way from their origins, who seek to bridge cultural divides and reconcile their individual experience with the complexities of an adopted culture.

Various exhibitions of the last decade have explored facets of Gauguin's career, illuminating specific periods and places. The present exhibition, the first major showing of Gauguin's work in London since the Arts Council's monographic exhibition held at the Tate Gallery in 1955 and the Tate's own Gauguin and the Pont-Aven Group of 1966, is also the first to attempt a new synthesis since the retrospective of 1988–9, held in Washington, Chicago and Paris. It views Gauguin's whole career through the suggestive contemporary lens of the narrative, both in terms of his crafting his own artistic myth and his propensity for appropriating stories and giving them new ambiguous meanings. It also reflects the artist's remarkable breadth of approach by including examples from every period, medium and genre.

Gauguin: Maker of Myth has been organised as a partnership between Tate Modern and the National Gallery of Art, Washington, which has lent most generously to the exhibition. The exhibition has been curated by Belinda Thomson, an acknowledged Gauguin scholar and curator of *Gauguin's Vision*, held at the National Gallery of Scotland in 2005, and Christine Riding, Tate Curator, with Amy Dickson, Assistant Curator. We would like to thank them all, in addition to National Gallery of Art Curator Mary Morton and Chief of Exhibitions D. Dodge Thompson, for meeting the many challenges of this project with such dedication, fluency and skill. The curators' acknowledgements detail the debts we owe to many collaborators and lenders of works of art to the exhibition. We would like to reiterate our thanks especially to the lenders, ever conscious that projects of this kind happen only through their sustained generosity and public-spiritedness. So widespread has this support been that it is perhaps unfair to single out a few in particular, but we would like to mention the British Museum, the Institut National d'histoire de l'art, Paris, and the Musée d'Orsay, who have lent so many important works from their collections.

Finally, we would like to acknowledge with gratitude the generous support of Bank of America Merrill Lynch, the exhibition sponsors for both London and Washington. Thanks are extended as well to the committed group of individuals and charitable foundations that have supported the staging of this exhibition at Tate as part of The Gauguin Exhibition Supporters Group.

ACKNOWLEDGEMENTS

Belinda Thomson and Christine Riding

Any exhibition on Paul Gauguin is greatly dependent on the research and writings of distinguished scholars, and we acknowledge in particular Scott Allen, Ziva Amishai-Maisels, Wayne Andersen, Alan Bowness, Richard Brettell, Françoise Cachin, Isabelle Cahn, Elizabeth Childs, Sylvie Crussard, Denise Delouche, Douglas Druick, Stephen Eisenman, Richard Field, Frances Fowle, Claire Frèches-Thory, Dario Gamboni, Martin Gayford, Suzanne Glover Lindsay, Gloria Groom, Anna Gruetzner Robins, June Hargrove, Martine Heudron, John House, Agnieszka Juszczak, Heather Lemonedes, Laurence Madeline, Victor Merlhès, Nancy Mowll Mathews, H. Travers Newton, Philippe Peltier, Ronald Pickvance, Anne Pingeot, Rodolphe Rapetti, George Shackelford, Charles Stuckey, Bogomila Welsh-Ovcharov, Eric Zafran, Peter Zegers. Along with many other scholars in the fields of literature and art, past and present, they have informed this exhibition and its texts. While developing our ideas over the last few years, the curatorial team had discussions with many people who were most generous in giving their time and expertise. In particular we would like to thank Caroline Boyle-Turner, Barrie Bullen, Guy Cogeval, Marie Cross, Ann Dumas, Elise Eckermann, Linda Goddard, Nancy Ireson, Mary Morton, Christopher Riopelle, Anne Roquebert, Richard Thomson and Alastair Wright.

Tamar Garb has played a dynamic consultative role, giving an invaluable overview to the exhibition's shape and the catalogue's scholarly arguments. We would also like to thank her and the other contributors to the catalogue, Philippe Dagen, Amy Dickson, Charles Forsdick, Vincent Gille, and Linda Goddard, for their important and illuminating essays. We owe an immense debt of gratitude to Vincent Gille for curating the documentary section and, once again, bringing to a Tate exhibition a unique historical dimension thanks to his specialised knowledge of French archives.

At Tate, we have benefited greatly from the advice and support of Nicholas Serota, Sheena Wagstaff, Matthew Gale and Vicente Todolí, former Director of Tate Modern. Three of our colleagues deserve special recognition: Achim Borchardt-Hume, now Chief Curator at the Whitechapel Art Gallery, who worked closely with Belinda Thomson as Tate curator until last year; Amy Dickson, who has had a significant role from the start, both curatorial and logistical, as well as being a contributor to the catalogue; and Maeve Polkinhorn, who has ably managed the documentary section. Other colleagues who have individually contributed to the successful realisation of this project are Nicola Bion, Simon Bolitho, Justina Budd, Elizabeth Buhe, Stephanie Bush, Iria Candela, Laura Clarke, Hannah Gruy, Richard Mason, Stephen Mellor, Helen Sainsbury, Minnie Scott, Emma Woodiwiss and Roz Young.

We are especially grateful to our colleagues at the National Gallery of Art, Franklin Kelly, D. Dodge Thompson, Mary Morton, Naomi Remes, Andrew Robison, Peter Parshall, Mark Leithauser, and Judy Metro as well as Jamé Anderson, Michelle Bird, Carol Christensen, Anabeth Guthrie, Ann Hoenigswald, Brad Ireland, Kimberly Jones, Lynn Matheny, Chris Myers, Nina O'Neil, Melissa Stegeman, Nancy Yeide and Deborah Ziska. We offer them all our sincere thanks.

A number of institutions and individuals have given their support to the exhibition. It would not have been possible without them. We would like to thank the following; Iman R. Abdulfattah, Helen Alexander, Mr and Mrs Joe L. Allbritton, Hope Alswang, Maxwell Anderson, Irina Antonova, Richard Armstrong, Maya Avelitcheva, Lázlo Baán, Joseph Baillio, Charles Bailly, Maria Balshaw, Jean-Luc Baroni, Stéphane Bayard, Christoph Becker, Idoya Beitia, Nadine Berthelier, Frederic Bigo, Regine Bigorne, David Bomford, Jean Bonna, Sandro Bosi, Antonia Bostrom, Heather Birchall, Ivo Bouwman, Howard Brevan, Rupert Burgess, Michael Bury, Bodil Busk Laursen, Connie Butler, Estelle Guille des Buttes-Fresneau, Caroline Campbell, Thomas Campbell, Olivier Camu, Véronique Cardon, Frédéric Casiot, Jean-François Cazeau, Catherine Chevillot, William J. Chiego, Michael Clarke, Melanie Clore, Guy Cogeval, Alfred and Ronald Cohen, Christofer Conrad, Peter Cooke, Stephen Coppel, M.I. Cordia-van der Lean, Martine Cornede, Sabine Coron, Caitlin Corrigan, Elizabeth Cowling, James Cuno, Penelope Curtis, Susan Davidson, Francine Dawans-Guidi de la Rosa, Nanne Dekking, Susan Foister, André-Marc Delocque-Fourcaud, Simon Dickinson, Anthony d'Offay, Michel Draguet, Douglas Dreishpoon, Annie Dufour, Ann Dumas, Flavie Durand-Ruel, Auden Eckhoff, Marie El Caidi, David Ellis, Valerie Eyene, Michele Fabre, Kaywin Feldman, Hartwig Fischer, Suzanne Folds McCullagh, Anne-Birgitte Fonsmark, Adrienne Fontainas, Philippe Fontainas, Frances Fowle, Flemming Friborg, Katharine Galitz, Mette Gauguin, Philippe Gauguin, Anna Genina, Marie-Jeanne Geyer, Leonard Gianadda, Lukas Gloor, George Goldner, Louis Grachos, Anne Gregerson, Deborah Gribbon, C. Griffith Mann, Antony Griffiths, William Griswold, Mireille Guillaume, Charlotte Hale, Tammy Harris, Jodi Hauptman, Frode Ernst Haverkamp, Lee Hendrix, William Hennessey, Tom Hewlett, Sally Hibbard, Clare Hills-Nova, Steven Hooper, Jane Houdek, Alan Howard, Colta Ives, Leo Jansen, Waldemar Januszczak, Annette Johansen, Samuel, Paul and Nina Josefowitz, Hervé Joubaux, Joachim Kaak, Serge Kakou, Mark Kernohan, Mary Kitson, Milan Knížák, Richard Koshalek, Dorothy Kosinski, Marc Larock, Joseph Lau, Eric Lee, John Leighton, Dominique Lelong, Heather Lemonedes, Thomas Lentz, Philippe Le Stum, Jean-Marc Léri, Gérard Lévy, Jenny Levy, Dominique Lobstein, Irene Lotspuch-Phillips, Glenn Lowry, Eric McCauley Lee, Neil MacGregor, Dale Mahar, Daniel Malingue, Joseph Marshall, Stéphane Martin, Caroline Mathieu, Rory Matthews, Vladimir Matveev, Marc Mayer, Bernhard Mendes Bürgi, Annie Metz, Cora Michael, Julie Milne, Charles Moffett, Dominique Morelon, Dahlia Moustapha, Aude Mouton, Christian Müller, Nathalie Muller, Isabelle Neuschwander, Jan Newton, Monique Nonne, Patrick Noon, Jean-Marc Pambrun, Michael Park-Taylor, Nicholas Penny, Aymeric Perroy, Ann Philbin, Estelle Pietrzyk, Hélène Pillu-Oblin, Paula Pineda, Mikhail Piotrovsky, Vincent Pomarède, Martine Poulain, Bruno Racine, Sylvie Ramond, Sean Rainbird, Christopher Riopclle, Joseph Rishel, David Rockefeller Sr., William Robinson, Malcolm Rogers, Jean-Yves Rolland, Anne Roquebert, Cora Rosevear, James Roundell, Tom Roundell, Timothy Rub, Axel Rüger, Willem D. Russell, Marie-Pierre Salé, Valérie Sax, John Scally, Scott Schaefer, Klaus Schrenk, Shannon Schuler, Anu Selvaraj, Livia Sevier, George Shackelford, Guillermo Solana, Kristen Sonniksen, Kathleen Soriano, Paul Spencer-Longhurst, Susan Stein, Nathalie Strasser, Deborah Swallow, Chikako Takaoka, Shuji Takashina, Michael Taylor, Matthew Teitelbaum, Alicia Thomas, Carmen Thyssen-Bornemisza, Gary Tinterow, Emmanuelle Toulet, Jean-Yves Tréhin, Peter Trippi, Ernst Vegelin van Claerbergen, Marije Vellekoop, Roger Ward, Malcolm Warner, Joanna Watson, James Welu, Uwe Wieczorek, Guy Wildenstein, Ully Wille, Georges and Sophie Winter, Veronika Wolf and Nina Zimmer. At Tate Modern the exhibition has been made possible by the assistance of the Government Indemnity Scheme, which is provided by DCMS and administered by MLA.

Lastly, Belinda Thomson wishes to thank her family for their encouragement and, above all, her husband Richard, without whose unwavering support she could not imagine having got through. The year 2010 will be one to remember, when Gauguin and Monet lodged temporarily side by side in Edinburgh.

9

Gauguin's Rupture with Impressionism

When Gauguin emerged as a new player on the French art scene in the early 1880s, the place of narrative in figurative painting was a contentious issue, affecting artists across a wide spectrum of practice, from the academic to the modern. For successful academic history painters such as Jean-Léon Gérôme (1824–1904) and Jean-Paul Laurens (1838–1921), and naturalist genre painters such as Jules Bastien-Lepage (1848–1884) and Émile Friant (1863–1932), underpinning the compositional structures of their carefully contrived tableaux were certain well-understood conventions they had been taught at the École des Beaux-Arts. Irrespective of whether the subject featured a scene from the *Odyssey* or Roman history, a north African slave market or a gathering of labourers in rural France, there would typically be centralised focus on a pregnant moment in the narrative, the key protagonists indicated by appropriate lighting and colour, telling interchanges conveyed through plausible, sometimes histrionic gesture and facial expression. If the resulting images, even when brought to a fastidious, quasi-photographic level of finish, suffered from a degree of staginess, the advantage was that the public instantly knew how to read the artist's meaning, especially when helped along by a title. That might be prosaically descriptive, teasingly piquant, or allusively poetic (fig. 2).

With Édouard Manet (1832–1883) in the 1860s and the advent of 'la nouvelle peinture', as Impressionism was dubbed in 1876 by Edmond Duranty, new narrative conventions came into play together with new subjects. In the hands of skilled figure painters – Edgar Degas (1834–1917) or Berthe Morisot (1841–1895) for instance – narrative did not disappear but took on more subtle guises. Particularly in genre (everyday life) painting, theatricality and rhetorical gestures were abandoned in favour of discreet low-key ways of infiltrating meaning, devices appropriate to the informality and intimacy of the chosen subject and the faster pace of modern life: typically, figures seen from awkward angles rather than head-on, placed off-centre or cut by the frame, their individuality characterised by telling details of costume or body language. In 1886 Seurat presented his major challenge to these narrative conventions of informality and naturalness when he deployed his static, ordered, frieze-like composition in *A Sunday on the Grande Jatte (1884)* (fig.3), in the process hinting at the artifice and formal posturing he saw in modern urban life. But resorting to extra-pictorial literary devices, requiring pictures to be read, was increasingly anathematised. Gustave Moreau (1826–1898), committed though he was to the traditional themes of history painting, roundly castigated artists who had recourse to literary tags and anecdotage instead of attending to the material business of painting.[20] The long-standing tradition of *ut pictura poesis* – wherein

the sister arts of poetry and painting, although constantly vying for dominance, were held to be interdependent – looked set to be toppled.

In his first efforts at composing modern landscapes and figure subjects, Gauguin was not tempted down the route of mainstream naturalism; he abhorred slick painting that had adopted a veneer of modernity but not fundamentally altered its mode of addressing the viewer, like the *plein-air* views of his own brother-in-law, Frits Thaulow (1847–1906).[21] If he went to the Salon and paid attention to its star turns, which he did, it was an incitement to do differently.[22] Claude Monet (1840–1926) and Paul Cézanne (1839–1906) were his heroes and Camille Pissarro (1830–1903) and Degas his chosen mentors: he imbibed their values along with their technical know-how. Like them, he was deeply suspicious of the 'literature of painting'.[23] Nevertheless, even during his years of exhibiting with the Impressionists from 1879 to 1886, Gauguin stood apart. For one thing he demonstrated from the outset that he would be exploring his artistic ideas in three dimensions: he worked as a sculptor, first in marble then carving directly in wood; from 1886 on, having been initiated by Ernest Chaplet, who gave him access to a kiln, he modelled pots and sculptures in clay which he regularly put on show.[24] Working in these three-dimensional media encouraged an alternative conceptualisation of the role of subject matter. The realism still evident in the first statuettes and portrait busts gave way to decorative, playful or symbolic combinations of motifs – figural types and animals – which he used to animate the surfaces of increasingly irregular-shaped pots (no.30). Furthermore, Gauguin's take on the genres of still life, portraiture, interiors and landscape was highly personal. Painting his children, as he frequently did, he betrayed a desire to enter into their imaginative worlds (*Clovis Asleep* 1884, *The Little One is Dreaming* 1881, nos.24, 25); and his still lifes regularly disrupt the expectations of the viewer, making the familiar feel strange.

The chaos caused to Gauguin's personal life by the abandonment of his financial career, his self-imposed exile from Paris, first in Rouen, then in Copenhagen, and the painful separation from his wife and children that ensued, only exacerbated a period of great uncertainty in his art. The new direction-seeking found expression in theoretical ideas about colour and line, nature and exaggeration, ideas that engaged with Impressionism but were also prescient of new directions. In his *Notes synthétiques*, drafted in a sketchbook used in Copenhagen, he explored the correspondences and differences between painting, literature and music, concluding – as Leonardo da Vinci had done – that painting was the pre-eminent art because the viewer was not expected

Fig.5 Camille Pissarro
Apple Picking 1886
Oil on canvas
124.5 x 124.5
Ohara Museum of Art, Kurashiki

to perform a feat of memory but could embrace the painter's meaning at a single glance: 'Like literature, the art of painting tells whatever story it wants but with the advantage that the reader experiences simultaneously the prelude, the mise en scène and the dénouement.'[25] But there was little sign at first of Gauguin putting such ideas into practice. In 1886 he turned his attention to rural peasant and landscape subjects in southern Brittany, a region to which he was drawn first and foremost for reasons of economy. Although he succeeded in contradicting the practice of the painstaking 'earthbound' naturalists by whom he found himself surrounded, initially he struggled to be other than derivative of Pissarro (fig.5).

It was in 1888, working alongside Émile Bernard and Vincent van Gogh, that Gauguin dramatically distanced himself from Impressionism and his art became distinctive and simplified in style, clearcut and powerful. He was bringing new stylistic sources into play – Japanese prints, children's book illustrations, *images d'Épinal* – and these served to unlock the promptings of his imagination. With the distinctive 'synthetist' style that resulted from this year of collaborative experimentation, in 1889 he went after public attention, seizing the opportunity to exhibit in Brussels and in M. Volpini's café at the Paris Universal Exhibition. Part of his challenge lay in presenting a new range of subjects. Indeed, the paintings, sculptures and ceramics of 1888–9 evoked Breton folk traditions, sinister undercurrents of rural sexuality. The Martinique subjects also, crucially, hinted at exotic worlds beyond France's borders.

In his writings, especially in his letters of the same period, Gauguin confidently and vociferously championed an art that went beyond material appearances, reclaiming those complexities of poetic meaning that had been lost in the great drive towards naturalism. The problem with Impressionism too, or so Gauguin believed, was that it was insufficiently intellectual. His old Impressionist comrade Armand Guillaumin (1841–1927), for instance, was incapable of responding to anything but ocular sensations, forgetting the part played in art by the brain; this was the reason he shrugged his shoulders at Gauguin's latest, more pondered, work.[26] What Gauguin was striving for – and admired in the work of others – was art that suggested something unseen, unknown. And he felt, in key works such as *Vision of the Sermon*, that he had achieved his aim. Paradoxically, he still craved the Impressionists' esteem. In 1891, on the verge of leaving France for Tahiti, he was desperate to know whether Monet approved of his 'evolution towards a complication of the idea through simplification of the form'. But could Gauguin really have expected Monet, whose principles he was now so openly flouting, to give his blessing to this blatant undermining of Impressionism? Monet was not to be so drawn.[27]

When Gauguin embarked upon the second half of his career, painting in the tropics thousands of miles from Paris, he had wrested from his Impressionist beginnings a mature, idiosyncratic approach to subject and style. Approaching the new Polynesian subject matter, he clearly felt his own master and able to control his responses to nature, free to heighten or simply reinvent where reality failed to match his dream. That alertness to the strange, the unexplained, the mysterious and symbolic – narratives that pervade his later work – had been a constant feature of his art, salient in the less familiar areas of his production, his ceramics and his carvings, but there too in the paintings that refused to be contained within the familiar appearances of reality.

Gauguin's Individual Use of Narrative
By his own admission the technical and aesthetic tendency of Gauguin's drawing and painting was to simplify form and colour – to seek out essential synthetic lines and shapes from the superfluity of detail in nature – in order to 'complicate the idea'. Thus, his art runs counter to the modernist tendency to evacuate meaning from painting, to tend toward flatness and non-representation. Looking closely at Gauguin's work and writings together reveals an artistic imagination of subtlety and complexity. In a plethora of ways he succeeded in insinuating into his work ideas that have an implicit or explicit narrative dimension, drawn from a wide variety of sources. For alongside the savage artist who wanted to go back to the beginnings of art was the artist who was attuned to the wit and fast-paced media of the boulevard and financial world,

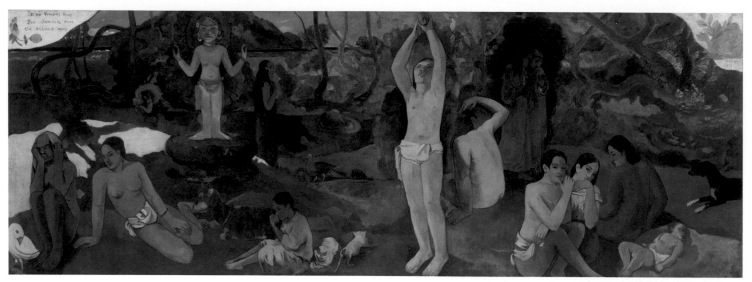

Fig.6 *Where Do We Come From? What Are We? Where Are We Going? (D'où Venons Nous / Que Sommes Nous / Où Allons Nous)* 1897
Oil on canvas
139.1 x 374.6
Museum of Fine Arts, Boston

who both admired the pathos in Rembrandt van Rijn's etchings *and* delighted in the succinct visual narratives and sardonic captions of Honoré Daumier (1808–1879) and Jean-Louis Forain (1852–1931).

Gauguin's own deployment of narrative was anything but straightforward. Sometimes it amounted to what one might call anti-narrative. Favourite ploys include hinting at half-understood goings-on through pregnant choices of motif or pose; having figures within the composition make eye contact and seemingly interrogate the spectator in portentous ways; imposing on the composition a suggestively loaded title, often framed as a question, yet leaving the interrelationships of the protagonists unclear. In *Aha oe feii (Eh quoi! Tu es jalouse / What! Are you Jealous)?* of 1892 (no.116), for instance, the figures' gestures are deliberate and pondered, but we do not know who is addressing whom. The regular inclusion in his compositions of Tahitian words was a way of simultaneously suggesting meaning but placing a barrier to its comprehension. Even when seeming to offer a verbal exegesis of a complex work, as Gauguin did on various occasions in letters sent to those likely to have to speak on his behalf, he often proffered an incoherent narrative, or promptly retracted what he had just said. He began to do this with the first difficult works of 1888 – *Self-Portrait, Les Misérables,* for instance, *Vision of the Sermon* and *Misères humaines* – and the practice continued to the end of his career when he engaged in a dialogue with André Fontainas over the meaning of *Where Do We Come From?* (fig.6). This teasing, provocative, take-it-or-leave-it attitude to meaning carried over into Gauguin's writing. Imposing such blocks to the viewer's fuller understanding was part of his renegotiation of a space in art for suggestive, but not explicit, narrative meaning. Operating within an avant-garde that disdained 'literary painting', Gauguin had to position himself with great care. In 1901 he told de Monfreid: 'I have always said, (or if not said) thought that the literary poetry of the painter was special and not the illustration or translation into forms of written texts.'[28] Quite possibly he had not said this, but Whistler had, in 1885 in the *Ten O'Clock* lecture.

Although inspired by nature, Gauguin defended his right to exaggerate his observations for artistic effect. His melancholic scenes of Breton rural life corresponded, he made clear, not to how Pont-Aven or Le Pouldu actually looked but to his own subjective vision. He wanted 'to suggest suffering without specifying what kind of suffering'.[29] This sometimes meant fusing experienced reality with pre-existing, cultural stereotypes: presenting Brittany as the land of superstitions and sad desolation. In 1893 Charles Morice felt the need to put viewers of Gauguin's first exhibition of images from Tahiti on their guard: 'to find your way around the *island* his work would make a bad guide, if your soul is not akin to his'.[30] If Gauguin's individual representations defied truth to appearances, within the work as a whole there was an overarching logic at work. Certainly, one quickly becomes aware of reprises, repetitions of an almost musical kind, recognisable poses that recur in different contexts. These sometimes take on the appearance of hauntings, personal obsessions, or leitmotifs, as in the case of the hooded figure seen in still lifes and Polynesian religious scenes (nos.23, 99, 101). With its revival of the great stories of Christianity, its appropriation and exploration of Polynesian – or what he called 'Maori' – legends, Gauguin's art regularly forged links with specific literary and cultural ideas. We see this in the self-portraits where his own features became those of Victor Hugo's hounded criminal Jean Valjean from *Les Misérables* (fig.1), the martyred John the Baptist (no.5), Christ in the Garden of Olives (no.9), or a satanic seducer (no.93). His nudes became Ondines, Eves, Hinas or Vairaumatis, his mothers became Madonnas, thereby evoking, consciously or not, that persistent Romantic myth of the Eternal Feminine. These works served as preludes to Gauguin's more ambitious engagement with the grand narrative topoi that characterise his later work – creation myths, subjects evoking fear, death and the supernatural, the myth of the Earthly Paradise. When the artist's career is viewed as a whole in this way, rather than in the discreet chronological or geographical segments that are often used to shape it, it can be seen as coherent and logical, as he maintained it was.[31]

The Pitfalls of Historiography

How, then, did Gauguin's art become coupled with the notion that to be modern, art had to set aside issues of subject matter? To understand this conundrum it is necessary to go back to the reactions of the young artists and critics he most profoundly affected. To them, Gauguin's synthetism seemed to imply nothing short of a redefinition of painting. In 1890 the twenty-year-old Maurice Denis published a theoretical manifesto entitled 'Definition of Neo-traditionism' in which Gauguin's recent art played a central role. Denis began with the arresting injunction: 'Remember that a painting, before it is a warhorse, a nude woman or some anecdote or other, is essentially a flat surface covered with colours arranged in a certain order.'[32] The phrase was intended to shock out of their complacency those who saw and judged art exclusively in terms of subject matter. Its uncompromising force led even Denis's closest peers to agonise about their painting, no longer sure what role the study of nature should be allowed to play, anxious about any temptation toward sentiment or story, anything that seemed to get in the way of purely formal concerns. Denis's motivation was a wish to persuade his readers of the plastic component of art's emotional expressiveness; he placed works such as Gauguin's *Breton Calvary* (no.67), for instance, and the contemporary murals of Puvis de Chavannes, greatly admired by Gauguin too, within a decorative tradition going back to the Italian primitives and the Egyptians. Yet though Denis's own commitment to an art that expressed his profound Catholicism was never in doubt and the extremism of his famous phrase was certainly never intended to open the door to abstraction, formalism took on a life of its own. Even as Gauguin was developing his complicated and allusive art in the South Seas in the later 1890s, the artist himself was anxious about being overtaken by history, feeling that his successful young supporters had in a sense moved the story on without him.

The formalist ideas of the 1890s gained a new international currency when the art critic Roger Fry organised an exhibition in London in late 1910 with the aim of introducing British audiences to the previously little-seen work of Gauguin, Cézanne and van Gogh.[33] Now rather too firmly defined as 'Post-Impressionists', they soon came to be seen as the cornerstones of modern art. At the inaugural exhibition of the Museum of Modern Art in New York in 1929, Gauguin was presented as an exemplar of High Modernism, side by side with Cézanne, van Gogh and Seurat. Hence the initial tendency to downplay the tale-telling aspect of Gauguin's art as a slight embarrassment, certainly an irrelevance. What mattered above all else was the freedom Gauguin claimed for artists to depart from the limitations of seen reality, to exaggerate the colour contrasts in nature, to simplify its forms, to produce a synthesis that stood as an equivalence for the artist's intense sensation. Fry's famous catch-all term, Post-Impressionism, legitimised in the 1940s and 1950s by John Rewald's documentary work, tended to put all the emphasis on formal shifts, rather than seeing content and form as of a piece. It is a style label, no more.

As with all radical shake-ups in art history, provoking such a reaction depended upon presenting a stark, caricatural case. But Fry subsequently showed himself to be

Fig.7 Exotic Eve 1890
Oil, gouache and mixed media on paperboard mounted on canvas
43 x 25
Pola Museum of Art, Japan

Fig.16 *Nègreries Martinique* 1890
*Gouache, watercolour, ink, gold paint
and collage on paper
33.2 x 24.8
Galerie Krugier & Cie*

posed local women who performed their roles as 'mulâtresses', 'négresses' or 'les belles Martiniquaises' against the familiar settings of palm leaves, cacti and fruit-filled baskets.[16]

For Vincent van Gogh it was the sensual overload of the landscape as the location for an unfamiliar and exotic cast of characters that was memorable in the two paintings of Martinique that he saw at his brother Theo's in 1888. Recalling a river-bed, purple mud, pools reflecting the 'pure cobalt blue of the sky, green grass', van Gogh described 'a negro boy with a red and white cow, a negress in blue, and some green forest'.[17] Intense colour and a specific figural type is what had stuck in the mind of this observer. In fact, the idea of the 'negro' as a signifier of this series is repeatedly invoked by successive commentators. And when Gauguin himself chose, two years after his visit, to invoke the island in a flattened synthetic design, he accompanied his easily identifiable figures – the women clad in characteristic colourful scarves and knotted headdresses – with the inscription '*Nègreries Martinique*', as if his new-found linearity, flattened style and arbitrary colouration could sit under the banner of this racially inflected inscription (fig.16). By 1889, when the experience of Martinique had already become a *souvenir*, Gauguin translated it into paintings, prints and figurines which encapsulate the racialised myth that was at the heart of his encounter with this place. The terracotta *Statuette of a Martinique Woman* (c.1889) has flesh painted a sonorous black. And amongst the prints of the Volpini suite are two images depicting a place peopled by 'négresses' arranged in statuesque poses and distilled into flattened, pictorial emblems nestling against the backdrop of an imaginary landscape (no.125).

Gauguin's almost exclusive concentration on African peasants and rural workers in his Martinique paintings is extraordinary, given the fact that the island was known to host one of the most diverse and mixed populations imaginable in the nineteenth century. In fact, it was the *créolité* of the island that Gauguin had already repressed, even before he went searching, as Glissant was to claim, for 'authenticity' elsewhere.[18] Lafcadio Hearn, on the other hand, took prurient pleasure in chronicling the permutations of identity produced by Martinican *métissage* at a time when theories of pure blood and untainted racial lineage were pervasive in Europe and the colonies. He described the island as having 'a population of the Arabian Nights', invoking the exoticising narratives of the orientalist and filtering his experience through an acculturated colour-coded lens: 'It is many-colored (*sic*); but the general dominant tint is yellow – yellow in the interblending of all the hues characterizing *mulâtresse, capresse, griffe, quarteronne, métisse, chabine,* – a general effect of rich brownish yellow'.[19] In a veritable inventory of the hybridised products of miscegenation, Hearn invokes the categories invented in francophone culture to accommodate and contain human variety. For Gauguin, such figures were of limited interest. It was not this melding of peoples and progeny, produced, for the most part, through the history of sexual congress between male slave owners and female slaves, that Gauguin pictured in oils. Nor was he much interested in depicting the large immigrant communities of Indians and Chinese who had been brought as indentured labourers to the island in the wake of the abolition of slavery in 1848, or the white colonials, the *békes*, from whom he kept his distance. Instead, Gauguin's paintings construct a coherent and mythic world – little found on the island at the time – a rural paradise, or 'Pastorales Martinique'[20] as he himself was to label it, comprised predominantly of African women accompanied by domestic animals and the occasional child or youth.

Soon after arriving with the painter Charles Laval at the bustling port of Saint Pierre on the west coast of Martinique, after a miserable sojourn in Panama, Gauguin wrote in a letter to his wife Mette: 'Right now we are living in a Negro hut (une case à nègres) and it's a paradise compared to the isthmus. Below us is the sea, bordered by cocoanut palms, above us, all kinds of fruit trees . . . Negroes and Negresses go about all day with their creole songs and their endless chatter; don't think its monotonous, on the contrary it is very varied . . . I can't tell you how enthusiastic I am for the life in the French colonies . . . Nature is at its richest, the climate is warm but with intermittent coolness'.[21] The echoes with Baudelaire are clear. Chattering locals, abundant nature, gentle weather conditions: these are the familiar fantasies that informed Gauguin's quest and which he was predisposed to paint. That Gauguin and Laval were 'slumming

Fig. 17 Rum Label
Print on paper
Musée Régional d'Histoire et
d'Ethnographie, Fort de France

it', to use Glissant's phrase, is clear. Choosing, in this highly segregated society, still structured around the production of sugar cane, to live in a simple cabin situated in a compound of impoverished black workers, the two painters were making an emphatic statement about where they placed themselves in the social structure of their temporary home. The *cases à nègres* were habitually two-roomed, wooden structures that had housed slaves on the smaller plantations, or *habitations*, which characterised the Lesser Antilles; and though slavery had been abolished in 1848, the social position and living conditions of workers had shifted little by the time Gauguin and Laval took up residence in their ramshackle quarters, set two kilometres from the town, near to the ocean and surrounded by fruit trees and plants. Presumably the only two Europeans to take advantage of the cheapness and availability of such accommodation, the painters must have seemed oddly misplaced to their bemused and inquisitive neighbours.

But the *case* did not only provide convenient and cheap accommodation for Gauguin. It also appeared as a structure in numerous works from paintings to fans and inscribed something of the specificity of this place (nos.42, 45). Crucially, its associations and location fed a number of fantasies that were generative for the work he would produce. Lafcadio Hearn, in his novel *Youma: The Story of a West Indian Slave*, set in Martinique and written during exactly the same period that Gauguin and Laval settled into their temporary home, describes the importance of these dwellings in Antillean folk tale and myth: 'The European cottage of folk-tale becomes', he declared, 'the tropical *case* or *ajoupa*'.[22] These structures, according to Hearn, provided the rich setting for Creole fairy tales of 'beautiful half-breed girls' who replace the familiar 'Cinderellas' and pale 'Princesses' of the European imagination with sultry Venuses and duplicitous devils, strikingly reminiscent of the 'half-nude *travailleurs*' with whom they are easily confused. The *case*, therefore, provided a locus of phantasmatic immersion: not only did it appear to be embedded, by its very material structure and situation, within the lush vegetation and sensual richness of the island, it also functioned as the perceived setting for the legends, folk tales and myths of its intriguing and mysterious inhabitants. That Gauguin's situation was fuelled by an unresolved desire for fusion or identification with the 'savage' sensibilities of his neighbours is encapsulated in a figurine he produced soon after his return to France. Revisiting the erotic and aesthetic orthodoxies of the classical tradition, Gauguin reworked the figure of Venus/Salomé in the form of a black woman, adorning her with headdress and earrings as well as the serpentine plant-life associated with this island paradise, but placing his own severed head, like a supplicant to some foreign deity, precariously in her lap (no.97).

Like Baudelaire who had invoked 'the chattering of little Negresses', Gauguin was, as we have seen, struck by the sounds and the speech of his adopted neighbours, which like the warmth of the Antillean breeze or the humidity of the air, appeared to suffuse and surround him. It was in the environs of his hut, near the paths through the mountain and along the beach where the famous *porteuses* (female carriers) promenaded and on the banks of the river where the *blanchisseuses* (laundresses) beat their washing against the stones, that Gauguin recognised his subjects. In this he was not alone. Countless photographs of the period capture just such figures who, as we have seen, had provided the favoured subjects of lithographs and prints for some hundred years. It was also these very types whom Lafcadio Hearn so graphically invoked, devoting lengthy chapters of his 'Martinique Sketches' to each and wondering at their deportment, movement and 'half-savage beauty'. Gauguin, too, expressed his fascination with the 'comings and goings of the *négresses* rigged out in colourful rags with their gracious and infinitely varied movements'.[23] Identified with the stock theme of the 'happy negress', Martinique had, by the mid-century, come to be viewed by the French as the home of a wholesome, natural femininity which was as much a product of the island as the sugar and rum that it exported. Indeed, it was this very image that was used to market its products. Before he had even left Paris, Gauguin would have seen images on trademarks, labels and advertisements for the famous island rum in which the familiar coast of St Pierre is accompanied by the costumed bust of this emblematic figure (fig.17). So when he emerged from his hut, sketchbook in hand, to draw the folk that he saw, Gauguin

Fig. 18 Tropical Conversation (Negresses Chatting) 1887
Oil on canvas
61 x 76
Private Collection

was already furnished with a set of internalised images and stereotypes that would delimit his choices and predispose him to certain figural constructions.

And it was to these that Gauguin turned, channelling his preconceptions into visceral encounters with models and sitters who would pose for the European stranger now residing amongst them. In pencil, pastel and crayon he drew his neighbours, picking fruit, doing laundry, sorting washing or sifting coal, seated thighs apart or walking with their loads held high on their turbaned heads (fig.18). Intrigued by their gestures and gait, he pictured the expressive hand-movements and characteristic stance of individual figures, sometimes isolating fragments, like the bare feet, outstretched limbs or spread-legged postures which were so foreign and fascinating to him. Only on one occasion did the sketch reach the status of a portrait, with the animated frontal address of the model and the unique gesture of the hand coexisting on the page with the coordinates of generalised typology (no.46). Mostly the faces are turned, screened or distanced, so that it is the costume and characteristics that define the figures as types. Gauguin's Martinican corpus revels in bodies saturated with difference. Though originating here, they would feed into a lexicon of poses recycled throughout his life. Uncorsetted, squatting or crouching close to the earth on which they sat or stood on their hardened soles, these bodies seemed, to the foreigner, unburdened by civilisation and the suffocating strictures of the society from which he had so recently fled.[24]

But Gauguin made decisive choices as to viewpoint and scene, models and motifs. Most noticeably, he created a world populated almost entirely by female figures, censoring out the labourers and fishermen who cohabited in his immediate surroundings. Not for him the 'half nude *gabarriers,* wont to wield oars twenty-five feet long; – the herculean *nèguegouôs-bois*, brutalised by the labor of paddling their massive and awkward craft; – tough *canotiers*, . . . the men of the cooperies, and the cask rollers, . . . the stowers; and the fishers of *tonne*, – and the fishers of sharks'.[25] Not for him the bustling activity of the port and the labour of the men who sustained it. Instead, Gauguin constructed an effortless, accommodating world in a nature so abundant and plentiful that it appeared to nourish rather than enslave its docile inhabitants, content like their farmyard animals to live out their simple existence. But in it, Gauguin felt his difference – without it how could he have painted? For all his desire to 'live as a savage', he remained profoundly aware of his identity as 'un blanc' ('a white man') and a 'European' amongst women of colour, and wrote to his wife of the need to defend himself against the flirtatious and predatory behaviour of the locals whom he described as 'les dames Putiphar' (invoking

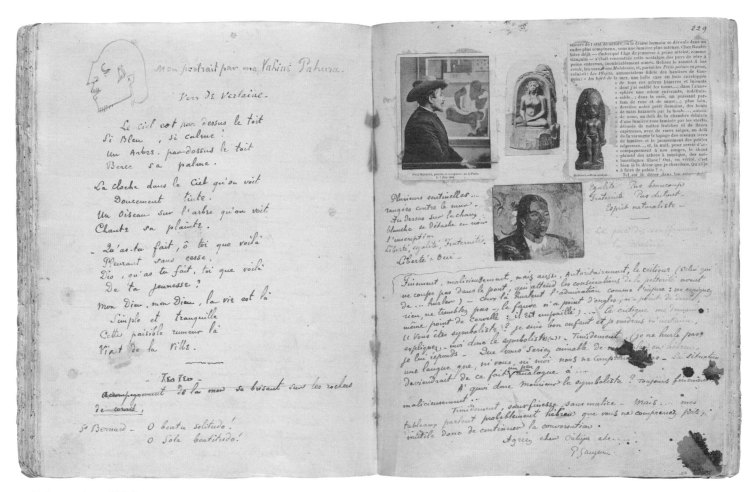

Fig.20 _Diverses choses_ 1896–8
pp.228–9, folios 117 verso, 118 recto
Manuscript notes and sketch,
pasted-in photographs and press
cuttings
Each page 31.5 x 23.2
Musée du Louvre, Département des
arts graphiques, Fonds Orsay

Despite Gauguin's prodigious output, most scholars have avoided these writings, viewing them as merely self-serving or confessional and accepting at face value Gauguin's denials of literary expertise.[8] Even those who have published editions or anthologies insist on the crudeness and simplicity of his prose, claiming that Gauguin 'was not a writer'[9] and 'lacked the essential strategies of rhetoric'.[10] In relation to _Noa Noa_, Jean Loize argued that 'As soon as he takes up a pen, Gauguin is entirely spontaneous, with no literary tricks: he knows that he is barbarous and shocking.'[11] In a recent monograph on Gauguin, Henri Dorra similarly described his writings as 'spontaneous and untidy' and 'hopelessly wordy and repetitious', while Richard Brettell concurred in his foreword that the painter 'fortunately, operated more fully in the realm of the visual than the verbal'.[12] This essay challenges these assumptions of naivety, arguing that Gauguin's writing is more sophisticated than has generally been supposed, and central to his artistic identity. In particular, it explores Gauguin's claim to 'write as I paint my pictures'. This is not to lend credence to his own suggestion that he wrote and painted with equal spontaneity – 'following my fancy' – but to argue that the apparent naivety of his writing was as deliberately constructed as that of his paintings and 'savage' persona.

'I am going to try to talk about painting, not as a literary man, but as a painter', Gauguin declared in _Racontars de rapin_. He went on to contrast the sterile erudition of the 'so-called learned critic', whose expertise amounts to the recollection of 'names in catalogues', with the unassuming knowledge of the artist, who, even with his 'special gifts', barely succeeds in 'penetrating the secrets of the masters'.[13] Gauguin's contrast between the critic as arrogant fact-gatherer and the artist as naive mystic parallels the confrontation that he staged between the corruption of European society and the purity of Polynesian culture. In his texts and paintings Gauguin constructed a mythical vision of Tahiti as a tropical paradise – at once unspoiled and possessing an undercurrent of savagery and sexual adventure – that was being destroyed by contact with civilisation. In a similar way he presented artists as the innocent victims of literary critics, those 'corrupt judges' whose preconceived ideas prevented them from understanding

33

alternative forms of expression.[14] Far from being 'natural', Gauguin's apparently uncalculated prose was designed to echo the 'primitive' qualities that he attributed to Tahiti, in contrast to the more polished techniques of professional writers. For to prove his point that artists were better equipped than writers to analyse works of visual art, in his own writing he needed both to display evidence of his superior insight and to emphasise at all costs its non-literary character.

In order to achieve this, Gauguin adopted a deliberately fragmentary style of writing that was intended to contrast with the 'erudite', 'logical' prose of the critic.[15] Using exactly the same words, he defined both *Avant et après* and *Diverses choses* – a still-unpublished appendix to *Noa Noa* – as consisting of 'childish things': 'scattered notes, without sequence like dreams, like life made up of fragments, and because others have collaborated in it'.[16] On the title page of *Diverses choses*, Van Gogh's sketch of his 1888 painting *La Mousmé* – a provençale girl cast as a 'Japanese' adolescent – accompanies this disclaimer, confirming Gauguin's emphasis on collaboration, naivety and primitivism.[17] Gauguin's suggestion that episodes in his texts are randomly grouped 'partly for personal relaxation, partly to assemble certain favourite ideas' is found in both *Avant et après* and in the preface to the first edition of his broadsheet *Le Sourire*.[18] If offered only once, this confession of literary inadequacy might be convincing as a genuine apology, but when repeated insistently from text to text, it evolves into a statement of intent. Indeed, at one point in *Avant et après* Gauguin developed the formula into a striking visual metaphor, evoking a prismatic harmony of fragments: 'Different episodes, numerous reflections, a few jests, appear in this volume, from who knows where, come together and retreat; a child's game, images in a kaleidoscope.'[19]

These qualities of fragmentation, collaboration and childlike spontaneity can be seen in one of several double-page spreads of collaged images and text in *Diverses choses* (fig.20). In an imaginary 'letter to the editor' at the bottom of the right-hand page, to which he has added his signature, Gauguin continued his attack on art criticism, mocking critics who seek to categorise and label artistic styles and movements. Yet on the same page he pasted several cuttings from a review by Roger Marx of his 1893 Durand-Ruel exhibition, which include photographs of himself and his artistic creations, undermining his claim that artists should defend their own work 'without the intervention of an interpreter'.[20] Gauguin succeeded in minimising this contradiction, however, by using a careful arrangement of text and image to shift the focus away from the context of European art criticism, and toward his affiliations with poetry and the 'primitive'. At the top of the left-hand page, a simplified, stylised self-portrait, falsely attributed to 'my vahine [mistress] Pahura', confirms his savage credentials. He has placed it above a transcription of the Symbolist poet Paul Verlaine's confessional poem from *Sagesse* (1881), 'Le ciel est, par-dessus le toit' ('The sky is, above the roof') – a poem celebrating freedom and the beauty of nature, written while Verlaine was in prison for shooting his lover and fellow poet Arthur Rimbaud.

When copying Verlaine's poem, Gauguin reversed the order of the last two stanzas, shifting the focus from the theme of wasted youth in the poet's closing lines to the 'simple and peaceful' life evoked in his penultimate verse. He had already made this link between Verlaine's poem and his own idyllic vision of the Tahitian landscape when he transcribed it above an 1893–5 watercolour (fig.21) depicting a figure crouching by a large tree at the seashore (recalling the tree that dominates Verlaine's first two verses). In *Diverses choses* the poem is followed by a reference to the twelfth-century Cistercian monk Saint Bernard of Clairvaux, quoting his paean to solitude: 'Beata solitudo, sola beatitudo' ('Blessed solitude, only blessing'). By placing his self-portrait at the head of the page, above these borrowed texts, Gauguin suggestively linked his own exile from 'civilisation' to the virtuous isolation of the pious monk or the incarcerated poet.

On the right-hand page, the pasted-in section of Marx's review juxtaposes one of Gauguin's cylindrical sculptures showing the Polynesian moon goddess Hina with a passage from Charles Baudelaire's prose poem 'Les Projets' (1857), evoking a tropical landscape, and directly compares painter and poet in terms of their rejection of materialism and experience of exotic travel.[21] In the cluster of photographs at the top Gauguin has placed an 1894 studio portrait of himself in profile – which closely mirrors

the profile of his 'savage' likeness on the opposite page – alongside his representations of Tahitian women. In this photograph he stands in front of the seated figure from *Te Faaturuma (Boudeuse / Brooding Woman)*, whose pose reflects that of the female Buddha in the reproduction of his *Idol with a Pearl* carving to the right; directly below, a cropped photograph of *Vahine no te Tiare (Woman with a Flower)* focuses attention on the androgynous face of the woman, whose contemplative demeanour echoes Gauguin's own static pose. Again, this arrangement visually cements his identification with the Tahitian figures. Together, these various textual and visual associations build up a multifaceted portrait of the artist as a 'poetic savage'. Using a variety of media, authorial voices and literary registers – aphorism, criticism, poetry, polemic – Gauguin avoided the linear logic and labelling of the critical writing that he despised, in favour of the suggestive and synthetic approach that he associated with visual art.

Although not all the pages of *Diverses choses* include this combination of text and image, it could be argued that Gauguin based the structure of his entire manuscript on the principle of collage. Lacking narrative development and coherence, it consists of a patchwork of borrowed texts (often adapted, misattributed, or unaccredited), juxtaposed with passages of his own writing – frequently repeated from earlier texts, and sometimes attributed to a fictional author. Across one double-page spread, for example, a pasted-in quotation from Baudelaire, advocating exaggeration and excess in art, is surrounded by a crude anecdote about mating birds, followed by a fake Oriental treatise in which Gauguin disguised his own thoughts on the importance of simplicity in art as the advice of the 'ancient Turkish painter Mani-Vehbi Zumbul Zadi'.[22] As the voices of his alter egos combine with the borrowed words of his heroes and contemporaries, snatches of verse or light-hearted sound bites are attributed to 'a woman', 'a saint', an 'inmate from Charenton [an asylum]', or introduced with the words 'which English author was it who said that . . .', as if to highlight the shared ownership and mutability of ideas.[23] Moreover, Gauguin's claim that 'the thought which guides my work . . . is mysteriously linked to thousands of others, whether my own, or heard from other people' is expressed thematically in the content of his borrowed material, including, for example, the writer Edgar Allan Poe's theory of the imagination as 'infinite, encompassing the whole universe',[24] or the composer Richard Wagner's celebration of the 'total art work' ('*Gesamtkunstwerk*'). Wagner's belief that the idea of a 'fecund union of all the Arts' corresponds to a nation's desire to recall 'the noble mystery of its origins' and be 'restored to its purest essence' chimes with the connection

Fig. 28 _Seaweed Gatherers_ 1889
Oil on canvas
87 x 123.1
Folkwang Museum, Essen

We would expect, then, at least a few of Gauguin's works to show a noticeable denunciation of the state of the world. Yet, as anyone interested in Gauguin's works will know, no such works exist. There is nothing of this kind in the landscapes and still lifes of his Impressionist years: the landscapes are mainly of the area around Vaugirard and the countryside and woods outside Paris without any reference to industry, unlike what can occasionally be seen in works by Monet, Guillaumin or Pissarro;[8] no greater engagement is offered by the still lifes, bourgeois interiors decorated with bouquets and comfortably furnished. The _Study of a Nude_ exhibited at the Salon des Indépendants in 1881 was so highly praised by Joris Karl Huysmans not because it depicted the working woman's condition but because 'It is a girl of our times, and a girl who is not posing for the gallery, who is neither lewd nor simpering, but is simply busy darning her clothes'[9] (fig. 26). Huysmans does not even allude to what is humble about this act, what it indicates about the model's modest living conditions. His only concern is with the rejection of academic idealism and the treatment of flesh and anatomy: 'what truth in all these parts of the body'. We would have expected the novelist of Parisian misfortune, of solitude and embitterment, to comment on the canvas's naturalist implications – but he does not and the occasion for establishing Gauguin as the painter of working people is missed.

Fig. 29 _Little Breton Girls by the Sea_ 1889
Oil on canvas
92.5 x 73.6
National Museum of
Western Art, Tokyo.
Matsukata Collection

The situation is scarcely different in Brittany. Although accounts of impoverished peasant life, the harshness of the times for fishermen and farm labourers are far from rare,[10] and although the themes of poverty and hard labour can be seen everywhere at the Salon thanks to the paintings of Jules Bastien-Lepage and Jules Breton, only a few of Gauguin's canvases painted in Pont Aven and Le Pouldu can be interpreted in this way. If the adolescents are naked, it is because they are bathing or wrestling in the grass. The women's dress does not indicate anything either, and if we put the religious question to one side – we shall come back to it later – Gauguin does not seem to be overly sensitive to the everyday life of those he frequented from 1886 to 1890. The shepherdess in _Breton Shepherdess_ dreams, and the figure of the pig keeper in _The Swineherd_ is less important than the landscape in which he is set (fig.27). The _Seaweed Gatherers_ could be seen as a counter example were it not for Gauguin's letter to Van Gogh in which he talks about the painting only in terms of composition and colour (fig. 28). We look in vain for the trace of any protest against the hard labour of these women, as much in the letter as in the canvas. Only one work, _Little Breton Girls by the Sea_, shows ragged, barefoot children with sad eyes – 'two poor girls', as Gauguin described them (fig. 29).[11] It remains to be determined whether the essential element in the artist's view is their _misère_ or their youth, already desperate, already deprived of its innocence. And, whatever the case may be, one canvas would still be insufficient to

establish a strong relationship between what Gauguin thought of contemporary
Brittany and the way he painted it.

What is interesting here is not so much the nature of the artist's political
thoughts as the fact that they seem to be confined to his correspondence and his
statements: their transferral into the painting does not seem to take place. At least it
does not take place in the expected way: through description and, possibly, satire.

Would it be any different in Oceania? The stances taken by Gauguin are as
vigorous – and public – when printed in *Le Sourire* or *Les Guêpes*. He quickly understood
that the rules were the same in the colonies as they were in the capital: the rule of 'How
much'. 'At the colonial prison, at the colonial hospital there are always these same words
"How much?" You are labelled soldier, sergeant, officer according to the weight of your
purse . . . Then death takes you by surprise, carries you off: and you are given a beautiful
white shroud, a piece of grey fabric, a filthy rag according to the weight of your purse . . .'[12]
The terrible age that, in 1890, he announced would come to Europe had spread to
Oceania: 'Civilised hordes arrive and plant their flag: the fertile soil becomes sterile,
the rivers dry up; it is no longer a continual party, but a continual struggle for life, and
unceasing toil.'[13] Ten years on, Gauguin was still writing along the same lines, adding
simply that contrary to what he thought before his arrival, Polynesia had not escaped
from the triumph of gold that 'rots' everything and from 'sweet progress' – sweet is
undoubtedly used here to mean its opposite. It would be easy to add other quotations
all confirming the artist's judgement upon Western capitalism in its colonial variant.

It would also be just as easy once more to object that the canvases, drawings,
engravings – not to mention the wooden sculptures – bear no confirmation of this point.
They contain no allusions to social and economic differences. Not that Gauguin doesn't
depict the Tahitian population he frequented and with whom he lived. But what he paints
is its acculturation, the invasion of Christian manners and morals imposed by missionaries
– most of reformed faith – and colonial civil servants: long dresses, Tahitian women
condemned to modesty and remorse, their sadness, their apathy, the deceitful ways of
behaving they have developed from their contact with the white man.[14] The portraits of
women and the 'genre scenes' that often allude to jealousy and deception in matters of love
bear witness to the introduction of notions such as sin and contrition unfamiliar to the
Tahitians until the arrival of the French. On the other hand, themes of labour or poverty
do not appear either in the works or in *Noa Noa*. Rather it is the opulence of nature, the
abundance of fruit and animals, the fabulous tuna fishing and the generosity of the
artist's neighbours that are the themes painted or written about again and again (fig 30).

However detailed it may be, the study of Gauguin's production during his periods of residence in Tahiti and the Marquesas Islands reveals nothing new on this matter, with the result that analysis is caught in a contradiction: the repeated and vehement political and social critique of capitalism and its colonial development on the one hand; and on the other the extreme rareness, if not absence, of works that correspond to this critique. This contradiction means we are obliged to examine the artist's political thought more closely, as it may be more complex than at first sight.

One text reveals itself to be decisive, the *Cahier pour Aline*, written in 1892, and reduced too often to only one of its fragments, the genesis of *Manao tupapau* 1892. It contains remarks on poverty: 'I have known extreme poverty that is to say to be hungry, cold and all that follows . . . But what is terrible about poverty, is the impossibility of working, of developing one's intellectual faculties. In Paris especially, as in big cities, the race for money takes up three quarters of your time, half of your energy.'[15] It includes heavy references to the Panama scandal – which concerned Gauguin all the more in that he was briefly employed on the digging of the canal. He first condemns the immorality and the indifference of corrupt speculators, investors and politicians. He concludes by agreeing with the opinion of all those who see proof in the scandal of a conspiracy between parliamentary democracy and financial speculation: 'The stock exchange, all speculation, should be abolished, on these moral grounds.' But the following sentence reads: 'And yet this same stock exchange and speculation are the pivots of our financial existence. Without them, modern society wouldn't be able to function.'[16] Thesis and antithesis come one after another without resulting in a third sentence, or synthesis, to resolve the contradiction.

This is not the only such case mentioned in the *Cahier pour Aline*. In the same passage Gauguin states first that he is a Republican. 'Long live democracy! It's all there is.' However 'philosophically', the Republic is a 'trompe l'oeil' and artistically a disaster: 'The democrats, bankers, ministers and art critics strike protective postures and yet they do not protect, haggling like fishmongers at the market. And you want an artist to be Republican! . . . If the artist cannot live, then society is criminal and badly organised.'[17] That an artist cannot live, the Impressionists – and Gauguin with them – are the proof: the Third Republic despises them, its institutions keep them in the background. Gauguin cannot consider democracy, which is in reality a plutocracy, as the best form of government.

What would be the best form? Communism, Anarchism? The hypothesis is not even considered. The answer is the opposite. It is contained in two arguments: 'Intuitively,' writes Gauguin, 'instinctively, without thinking, I love nobility, beauty, elegant taste and the old saying "Noblesse oblige." I like good manners, even the politeness of Louis XIV. I am then instinctively, without knowing why, an ARISTO.' Intuition is followed by historical reasoning: 'As an artist. Art is only for the minority, it must itself be noble. Only great lords have protected art out of instinct, duty, and pride maybe. Anyhow they have made great and beautiful things happen. The artist was treated as an equal, so to speak, by kings and popes.'[18] Surprising sentences and a clear regret: he gives himself free rein as much on an autobiographical level, 'by instinct', as on a historical and artistic one – by citing Louis XIV, Michelangelo and Julius II, Titian and Philip II. Modern society is reprehensible, therefore, because it enslaves people to the humiliating power of money, replacing all previous relationships by the law of 'how much'. The purpose of this critique is not, however, to prepare the advent of a new, egalitarian and more democratic world. On the contrary, it is based on the admiration of, and regret for, a past era of aristocrats who knew how to treat artists and who did not haggle over their works like 'fishmongers at the market'. It is in no way a question of decadence but of the disappearance of one social and political system and of the dominance of another. It would be right to use the term 'reactionary' rather than conservative to define these reflections, to the extent that they are a reaction to the actual state of things in order to promote a vision – certainly idealised – of a previous lost state. The following somewhat undemocratic maxim can be found once again in the *Cahier pour Aline*: 'Great monuments have been built under the reign of potentates. I believe that great things too will be done only with potentates.'[19]

A previous lost state: it is easy to recognise one of the artist's essential themes in these words, so essential that his love for 'primitives' of whatever kind cannot be separated from it. This is obvious in Oceania. In *Noa Noa*, concerning the death of King Pomare V on Tahiti, Gauguin writes: 'There was one king less, and with him disappeared the last remains of Maori customs. It was well and truly over, nothing left but civilised people. I was sad: to have come so far for ...'[20] He makes the same remark concerning the Marquesas Islands: 'And so we witness this sad spectacle which is the extinction of a race for the most part consumptive, with infertile loins and ovaries devoured by mercury. In seeing this, I am led to think, or rather dream, of that moment when everything was absorbed, dormant, annihilated in the sleep of the first age, its infancy budding.'[21] In this way Gauguin condemns colonialism less for the oppression and injustice of which it is guilty,[22] than for its destruction of traditions and even the genetic patrimony of the native populations. Artistic primitivism, even though it appeared to be a revolutionary avant-garde aesthetic, was a response to this regret and to the destruction of bygone societies. This process was taking place as much in Europe, where the bourgeoisie had defeated the aristocracy, as in the tropics where the colonial regime had destroyed the old world and the 'old Maori cult'. Although the situations were very different in Paris and in Papeete, what the artist was witnessing were the consequences of a general change, the destruction of previous structures and social habits and the constitution of a new order based on money.

Feeling himself 'by instinct' to be an 'ARISTO', Gauguin can only be infuriated by this change which is so global that it affects even the Pacific Islands, just as he can only witness the loss of the Marquesan 'race' with sorrow, because to be Marquesan, as with being 'ARISTO', is a question of birth – a question of 'nobility'. Naturally, his socialist grandmother Flora Tristan was a 'noble lady'[23] and his mother herself a 'very noble Spanish lady'.[24] It is not for nothing that Gauguin depicts in such terms his childhood in Lima and his family tree in *Avant et après*. These tales explicitly place him within the old social system, and the ruin of his Peruvian family was a question of money and the stock exchange,[25] and as such it was a bourgeois drama typical of the bleak nineteenth century. In these autobiographical texts Gauguin rewrites his destiny in such a way that it coincides with his general political and historical theory.

The paintings and sculptures from these two sojourns in Oceania fit logically into this system. If, as already mentioned, a few allude to the acculturation of the Tahitians, to the change in manners and dress, the wooden sculptures, the mythological canvases and *Ancien culte mahorie* are attempts to recognise, restore and repair the irreparable damage of modernity. 'Would I succeed in finding a trace of that so distant and so mysterious past? And the present had nothing worthwhile to say to me. Finding the old hearth, reviving the fire in the midst of all these ashes. And doing this all alone,

*Fig. 31 Ancien culte mahorie 1892–3
pp.12–13, folios 6 verso, 7 recto
Watercolour, pen and ink
21.5x 17 (book)
Musée du Louvre, Département des
arts graphiques, Fonds Orsay*

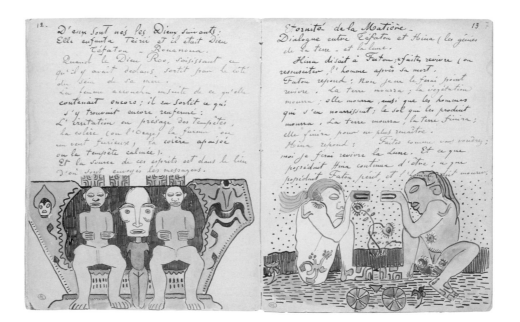

without any support.'[26] These sentences from *Noa Noa* clearly state the archaeological aspect of primitivism: the 'arrangements' of Tahitian, Marquesan, Kanak, Buddhist or Japanese references are an attempt to evoke a bygone age, lost cultures. Primitivism is an aesthetics of looking back. It must be accepted that it owes its aesthetic modernity to this desire for the past, and that it is deeply hostile to the Western world's material and social modernity, to its technical progress and to the advent of a new social order. We must admit that it embodies this paradox: an anti-progressive avant-garde that is simultaneously and dialectically revolutionary and counter-revolutionary.

The term 'lost cultures' has just been mentioned: the adjective brings to mind the 'lost paradise' of the biblical tales, the more so in that Gauguin deals with this explicitly in his painting *Te Nave Nave Fenua* and the variations on paper associated with it (nos.105, 103). There are other Christian motifs in the Oceanic style to add to this, which brings our analysis back to Gauguin's position on religion. The author of *L'Église catholique et les temps modernes* and *L'Esprit moderne et le catholicisme* is reputed to have been the bitter enemy of missionaries, clerical authorities and the enforced evangelisation of the natives. Seen from this angle, religion is only one of the instruments of acculturation, that is, the establishment of a new order. Religion or the Church? Gauguin does not confuse the two. His critique is addressed to the Church, its hierarchy and its priests as the abettors of the new social order, of 'modern society: . . . people who from earliest childhood suffer from *misère*, the contempt of others and to whom the priest offers, as sole compensation and consolation, absolution, happiness in paradise, all of which is guaranteed by the State.'[27] We can easily find hundreds of similar quotations denouncing the Church as tyrannical, deceitful and extremely rich. This modern Church goes 'against the grain of true biblical doctrine and Christ'.[28] So we must not confuse 'in our repugnance, Christianity with (the Church) which claims to be identical to it, its traditional, privileged and infallible interpreter, whereas it was only ever its doctrinal misinterpreter and was practised in the wrong way'.[29]

On several occasions Gauguin the anticlerical, the scourge of corrupt and corrupting bishops, evokes the early years of Christianity and the archaic Church in contrast to modern clergy. It is not surprising therefore that, just as he tried to breathe new life into Polynesian myths, he also attempted to rediscover the way to a Christian art worthy of early Christianity's fervour. In 1888 he wrote to Van Gogh about the *Vision of the Sermon*: 'I think I have reached a great rustic and superstitious simplicity in my figures.'[30] The painting was rejected by the priest of the church to which Gauguin wanted to give it – 'naturally'[31] rejected, he writes to Émile Schuffenecker. Why naturally? Because this 'superstitious' conception of religion already belonged to the past, just as firmly as European aristocratic society and 'Maori' culture did. Running so counter to modern society, all efforts to revive the emotions and customs of past centuries and the old aristocratic world could only ever be doomed to misunderstanding or hatred.

Translated by Anna Hiddleston

THE LAST ORIENTALIST: PORTRAIT OF THE ARTIST AS MOHICAN

Vincent Gille

Fig.32 Self-portrait as an Indian
Detail from a sheet of sketches
1889
Charcoal on paper
19 x 30
Current whereabouts unknown

We have a large orchestra, a rich palette, a variety of resources. We know many more tricks and dodges, probably, than were ever known before. No, what we lack is the intrinsic principle, the soul of the thing, the very idea of the subject. We take notes, we make journeys: emptiness, emptiness! We become scholars, archaeologists, historians, doctors, cobblers, people of taste. What is the good of all that? Where is the heart, the verve, the sap? Where to start out from? Where to go? We're good at sucking, we play a lot of tongue games, we pet for hours: but – the real thing! To ejaculate, beget the child![1]

At the dawn of the twentieth century, in a place far from Europe, Gauguin's light went out. At the same moment, many nineteenth-century constructions of the 'Orient' also passed away: constructions created and made manifest, most notably, by the poet's pen, the painter's brush, explorers' tales and (more sinisterly) the military might of colonial expansion. To understand Gauguin as an Orientalist, here, is not to force him into a category to which he clearly does not belong – a school of painters that he himself called 'ethnographers'. It is to suggest that the impulse that drove him to travel for his art – whether it be to Pont-Aven, to Martinique or to Oceania – makes most sense in relation to the ways in which, from the 1820s to the last decades of the century, painters and poets left their homes to seek the colours, sounds and syntax of a real or imaginary 'Orient'. Perhaps we can best understand this desire to escape, to go to the ends of the earth, in the light of the ways in which the 1880s and 1890s set up a paradoxical dichotomy between the 'near' and the 'far': between Paris and the 'exotic', 'untamed' places that the city dreamt up and dramatised in its spectacular exhibitions. The here and there, the real and the imaginary, the mundane and the mythical, the civilised and the savage ... (fig.32) permeable and changeable, the categories through which Gauguin weaved his

Fig. 33 Young Women in Traditional Costume in Pont-Aven
Musée des Civilisations de l'Europe et de la Méditerranée, Marseille

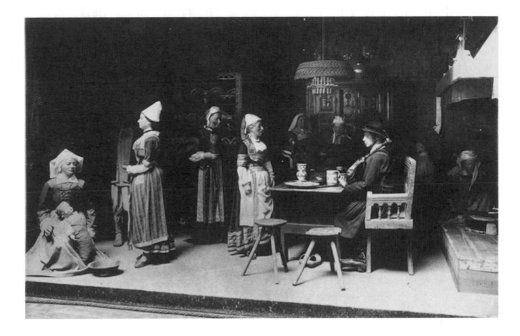

way were more present than ever in the spirit of the times. Between the far-off fantasies in which he got lost, seeking his way, and the countries whose characters and contours he tried to grasp, there is a middle ground where imaginary and real journeys, paradise and disenchantment come together. My text aims to follow him to the heart of that territory, tracing the steps of early nineteenth-century poets and travellers, ones who kept pace with their painterly and literary companions.

A Detour

In Paris, in January 1829, the young Victor Hugo published his second volume of poetry: *Les Orientales*. If its offerings were in keeping with the 'spirit of the times',[2] as their author himself observed, for their first readers, they had a poetic tone and brilliancy that were entirely new. Therein Hugo introduced a palette of novel sonorities, with an original vocabulary, handling unusual rhythms with distinctive brilliance. But the metaphors he used and the images he brought into play – from the predictably cruel Turkish warrior, to the ravished woman and the lascivious odalisque – were conventional nonetheless. This dabbling with the 'Orient' was an excuse to play with words, sounds and lights, to reveal great violence and diffuse eroticism. The 'Orient', in this scenario, was merely incidental: an ornament, a box of tricks containing all manner of sensations and landscapes. What mattered, then, was a question of aesthetics. The words were more important than the setting in 'This useless book of pure poetry',[3] as Hugo apologised in his preface.

Beyond the dazzling colours, sounds and rhythms, Hugo's poems introduced unusual narrative modes that disrupted traditional prosody: a succession of hypothetical questions in 'La Douleur du pacha', the repetition of one or several lines, like a refrain at the end of stanzas in 'Chanson de pirates' and 'Marche turque', a counting rhyme in the form of a wish in 'Voeu', or a curse as in his 'Malédiction'. The origin of these new ideas lay in popular Greek songs or Persian poems, medieval fables, oriental tales and Spanish romances. Hugo's recourse to these 'exotic' and popular sources, rich in 'naïve' imagery, unusual rhythms and original narrative modes, enabled him to break with the traditional forms and rhythms of epic poetry. This is characteristic not only of the *Orientales* but of romantic poetry in general: 'In the narrative poem, Romanticism, because it challenges old models, because it discovers new ones in what it naively calls "popular tradition", undertook research which was inconceivable up until then, into the construction of both the story and the narrative.'[4]

Gauguin and some of his circle at Pont-Aven had a similar approach when, in an attempt to break free from naturalism and Impressionism, they looked to the formal inventions of Japanese prints or *images d'Épinal* (popular nineteenth-century prints showing idealised scenes of French life); likewise when they attempted to absorb the

49

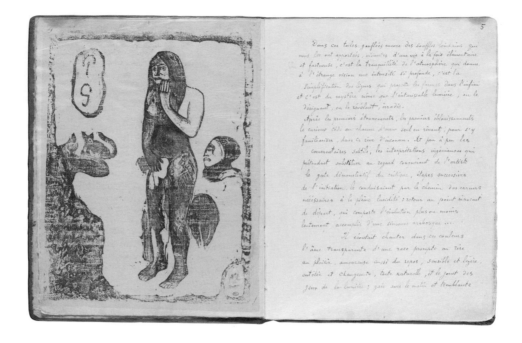

'character of the people and the country'.[5] 'I love Brittany', wrote Gauguin, 'I find the wild and the primitive here. When my clogs resonate on this granite ground, I hear the muffled, powerful thud that I'm looking for in painting.'[6] Brittany was perceived at the time as the place in France where popular traditions were still at their most vital, even if they were heading towards extinction (fig. 33). The room dedicated to Europe at the heart of the Ethnographic Museum that opened in Paris in 1884 presented, in particular, a reconstructed Breton house (fig. 34): 'The models of men and women that animate this interior are dressed in full contemporary costumes, several of which, though commonplace formerly, are dying out. Next to this group, [Breton] ethnography is represented with other costumes, including an intricate bride's gown decorated with sequins, some very curious christening bonnets, headdresses, etc.'[7] So Gauguin's approach can be understood as a comparable desire to enrich painting through 'naivety', straightforwardness, the direct transcription of immediate sensations and the appeal to the supernatural: the characteristics of popular tradition. And just as the aim of Hugo's volume of poetry was perhaps neither Orientalism nor exoticism, Gauguin's overriding priority – beyond his Breton, Martinican or even his Tahitian settings – seems to have been to bring about a fundamental formal and poetic shift. He did so by finding, via popular tradition, 'a lost paradise of poetry, which is a place of total light and total simplicity'.[8] Or, as he put it: 'I think I have attained a great rustic and *superstitious* simplicity in my figures.'[9]

Fables and Fantasies

Unlike Hugo, who dreamt of an 'Orient' he never visited, Gauguin travelled constantly. Back in France, he made his first journey the subject of a narrative of sorts; the subtitle of his *Noa Noa* is *Voyage à Tahiti*, which aligns its author with the great literary tradition of *Voyages* typified by, amongst others, François-René de Chateaubriand, Alphonse de Lamartine and Gustave Flaubert. Here I would like to pause for a moment to consider the extraordinary *Voyage en Orient* that Gérard de Nerval published in a series of articles between 1844 and 1850, and which he then brought together in a volume in 1851, several years after the journey itself of 1843.[10] Though it conveys a magical sense of homogeneity to the reader, in effect, Nerval's *Voyage en Orient* is a collection of fragments: a collage of what he had seen and what he had read. '[Nerval] saw less than he read. Often he saw thanks to books alone. Sometimes he makes us see what he had not seen, without making the difference between what he had read and what he had actually seen apparent.'[11] And just as, for example, the Cairo wedding procession that Nerval described was in fact based on information he gleaned in libraries,[12] the mythological tale Gauguin presented as having been told to him by his mistress – *Ainsi parlait Tehamana* – has its roots in the 1837 *Voyage aux îles du grand océan* by Jacques-

Exposition Universelle
PARIS 1889

Pagode d'Angkor

Antoine Moerenhout. The *Noa Noa* manuscript is a yet more varied collage of things seen, read, borrowed and – in Gauguin's case – drawn. In the manuscript, to the text that constitutes the narrative, he added photographs, reproductions of artworks from all sources, drawings, woodcuts – these combined with biographical fragments, souvenirs, sketches and mythological tales. Nerval and Gauguin wished to recreate, each in his own way, the full sensory and intellectual experience of a *journey* that plunges the traveller into other landscapes, languages, customs and belief systems. Their texts were designed to 'speak' in the first person; therein the authors presented their own memories or transformed them through the inclusion of imported material. Gauguin interspersed his narrative with descriptions of paintings; but these appear seamlessly, as if the depicted scene had really taken place.[13] The addition of numerous woodcuts or drawings links the artwork to the journey inextricably (fig. 35). Travel and the creative process are intermeshed; as if what was painted had really been *seen* and experienced. If Nerval, travelling as a poet, created a poetic work, Gauguin – the painter – created one that was essentially painterly.

Correlations can also be drawn between the references to what he called 'Maori' mythology that Gauguin integrated into his story and the legends and mythical tales that (on three occasions) punctuated Nerval's traveller's tale. This provokes a dualistic reading, which on the one hand links the journey to the narrator's contemporary life, and on the other connects it to an Arcadian past, to some kind of Eden before the fall. Thus the journey becomes an initiation. In the words of Nerval: 'Truly, I had already felt that in setting foot upon this mother earth, in re-immersing myself in the revered sources of our history and our beliefs, I would stop the passing of my years, that I would be a child once again in the earth's cradle, still young at the heart of this eternal youth.'[14] As for Gauguin, he seemed to find a piece of this far-off paradise in Tahiti: 'Everyday life – Tehamana opens up more and more. Docile, loving; the Tahitian noa noa perfumes everything. I am no longer aware of days and hours, of Good and Evil.'[15] Likewise he talked of *rejuvenation* as he left the island: 'Adieu, hospitable soil. I leave with two additional years – feeling twenty years younger, more barbaric and yet more learned.'[16] But this 'barbarism' must be understood as something rather different: as a search for material and spiritual harmony. 'There, in Tahiti, in the silence of beautiful tropical nights, I shall be able to listen to the sweet murmuring music of my heart's movements in loving harmony with the beings around me. Free at last with no money troubles and able to love, sing and die.'[17] Hence Gauguin's journey acquires one of the characteristics of voyages to the 'Orient' that, since the beginning of the nineteenth century, were always a return to origins, a nostalgic dream of a paradise lost, 'a flight back to the country of the sun, to the cradle of humanity, that is to say towards the Orient, to bathe in the very source of the mystery of creation and eternity, to be reborn under the sign of the sun'.[18]

Journeys and Disenchantment

After Nerval, but in his shadow nonetheless, Charles Baudelaire and Gustave Flaubert introduced the idea that the journeys we undertake can never live up to our dreams. This gap was to grow as the century advanced as, increasingly, the imagined heavenly 'elsewhere' was found to be almost identical to one's place of origin. And when presented there, in Paris, this mythical destination transpired to be full of mirages. Pierre Loti's novels, the articles and illustrations of the *Tour du monde* and the *Journal des voyages*, the huge success of exhibitions and the extraordinary displays of the International Exhibitions, contributed to the belief that the world was within easy reach, that the most distant place could be brought quite literally to the pavements of Paris.[19] 'It is a fairy-tale. But a fairy-tale without parallel. All colours, all forms of monuments are there to charm you ... As far as one can see are domes, bell-turrets, minarets, towers. A kind of unparalleled joy reigns over the ensemble. The eyes know not where to settle, since there are solicited from all angles, and we are tempted to run after the brightest [things], no longer knowing where they are. We walk in a dream', wrote Camille Debans in *Les Coulisses de l'exposition*.[20] Thus an all-encompassing syncretism was added to the now-familiar exoticism: all the world's eras, styles and forms were condensed into a few square kilometres (fig.36).[21] 'You were wrong not to come', wrote Gauguin to Émile Bernard of the 1889 International Exhibition. 'In the Javanese village, there are Hindus. All the art of India can be found there and the photographs I have of Cambodia can be found there replicated perfectly.'[22]

So Gauguin found in the literature of his time (travel journals, exotic novels and official propaganda), and in the colonial section of the 1889 International Exhibition, the images of his desire for elsewhere if not the source. ' ... Under a winterless sky, on marvellously fertile soil, the Tahitian only has to reach up his arms to gather his food – and so he never works', wrote Gauguin to the Danish painter Jens-Ferdinand Willumsen. 'While in Europe men and women satisfy their needs only after relentless labour, whilst they struggle in convulsions of cold and hunger, tormented by poverty, Tahitians, on the contrary, as happy inhabitants of the unknown paradise of Oceania, are familiar only with the sweetness of life. For them, living consists of singing and loving (conference on Tahiti by Van der Veene)' (fig.37).[23] This completely idyllic description is copied almost verbatim from the 1889 Colonial Exhibition's official handbook, which offered an enchanting description of Tahitian women taken from the same conference speaker. The text continued in the same tones: 'Born under a winterless sky, on marvellously fertile soil, the Tahitian only has to reach up his arms to receive the bread tree fruit and the féhi which constitute the basis of his food.'[24]

Gauguin's 'Orient', if enlarged to include the French Colonial Empire,[25] functioned as an antidote to his hatred of European civilisation. His desire to get away smacks of escapism: 'May the day come (and maybe soon)', he wrote to his wife Mette, 'when I can run and escape into the woods of an Oceanic island, living there on rapture, calm and art. Surrounded by a new family, far from this European struggle for money.'[26] And so he left, and he left on exactly the same terms as would an Orientalist painter: supported by an official mission,[27] and with the idea that he would for a certain time garner 'documents' to feed his work. 'When I come back I will have enough to satisfy customers ... I feel I am beginning to grasp the Oceanic character and I can assure you that what I am doing here has never been done by anyone else and is unheard of in France.'[28] Furthermore, at first, his journey appeared to live up to the expected enchantment: 'I am writing to you this evening. The silence of the night in Tahiti is even stranger than the rest. It exists only here, without a bird cry to disturb the peace ... The natives often move around at night, but barefoot and silently. Always this silence. I understand why these people can stay sitting for hours, for days, without speaking a word and looking melancholically at the sky. I feel that all of this will take me over ...'[29] These words are reminiscent of the Baudelaire of *Les Projets*, where a character describes an engraving: 'By the seashore, a fine wood cabin, surrounded by all those bizarre, gleaming trees whose names I've forgotten ... in the air, that intoxicating,

Fig. 37 Charles Georges Spitz
Fishing Scene near Afaahiti,
Tahiti c.1889
Photograph
Serge Kakou Collection, Paris

Fig. 38 Jules Agostini
Gauguin's house in Tahiti
Photograph
Musée du Quai Branly, Paris

indefinable scent . . . around us, beyond the room lit by the pink light filtering through the blinds, cool braided mats and sensual flowers . . .'[30]

But it was only a dream. Quite clearly, the liberating journey – the one to resolve all problems, widen horizons, the one that would reveal and satisfy the 'savage' self – did not unfold as planned. It is possible that this 'savage' heart, like the 'savage' people exhibited on the outskirts of Paris and at the Esplanade des Invalides, was itself an illusion: a decoy, a perverse invention that might serve to justify the process and progress of colonisation.[31] The 'elsewhere' that Gauguin hoped for so desperately did not exist, could not exist; contained by colonisation, it had disappeared entirely. 'The Tahitian soil is becoming entirely French', he wrote to Mette upon arrival, 'and little by little the way things used to be will disappear entirely.'[32] So disenchantment overtook Gauguin fairly quickly, a disenchantment common to a good many writers in the second half of the nineteenth century, as they too awakened to the realisation that the 'Orient' was but an illusion. To quote Nerval, for example: 'In sum, the Orient does not come close to that waking dream I had of it two years ago, or rather, that Orient is even more distant and unattainable. I have had enough of running around after poetry; I think it is on your doorstep, or perhaps in your bed. I am still a man who runs around, but I am going to try to stop and wait.'[33]

Painting, Exile

Perhaps after all, painting, like poetry, is not to be found at the ends of the earth. To his wife who reproached him for distancing himself from Paris, the supposedly real artistic centre, Gauguin replied: 'My artistic centre is in my mind'.[34] He already said of his stay in Martinique (my emphasis): 'The experience I had in Martinique was crucial. I only really felt *myself* there and it is in what I brought back from there that you should look for me, if you want to know who I am, even more than in my Brittany works.'[35] Beyond its location, painting is therefore *also* the result of an inner desire – 'what I desire is a corner of myself that is still unknown', he explained to Émile Bernard.[36] Gauguin, who never stopped describing himself as a savage, an Indian, a primitive, perhaps discovered, in an 'Orient' that was not so much exotic as created in direct opposition to the hated West, an understanding, a mysterious harmony, comprised of light and spirit, colours and perfumes, 'one of the greatest spiritual riches that I came to look for in Tahiti'.[37] Just as in *Les Orientales* Hugo created a work of poetry above all else, and just as Nerval, when writing his *Voyage en Orient* sought, beyond anecdote and simple narrative, truly mythical material within which to inscribe and understand his own life, it may be that Gauguin, by and in his work as a painter, thought to capture an authentic Orient which dwelt within himself, one that he could bring to light because he recognised what he saw. For the Oriental dream is, indeed, a dream, that is to say an inner journey. 'Man cannot change the depths of his heart. Exterior objects can distract him for a moment, but what will occupy him continuously and present itself to him continuously is his inner self, the

familiar dreams of his soul. After wandering around outside of himself for a while, he will, so to speak, go back into his heart.'[38]

Gauguin returned to Paris. The topic of his travelling, exile and exotic works had been effective forms of promotion, and they were used as such by his fawning admirers and preface-writers. At the time of the painter's first departure in 1891, Octave Mirbeau had written: 'I hear that M. Paul Gauguin is leaving for Tahiti. He intends to live there alone for some years, to build his hut and work anew on the things that haunt him. I found the idea of a man voluntarily fleeing civilisation in search of oblivion and silence in order to feel better, to hear better the inner voices that suffocate in the hubbub of our passions and arguments, both curious and disturbing . . .' (fig.38).[39] Gauguin's insistence on giving his works Tahitian titles, his extravagant costumes, his relationship with Annah la Javanaise, his studio in rue Vercingetorix decorated with Tahitian objects and accessories, all of this combined during his last stay in Paris to highlight his exiled, barbarous, wild character. However, between Gauguin's first and second trips to Tahiti there was a marked difference. The first, which can still be seen as the typical Orientalist undertaking, was only a *journey*. The second resembled an exile – due to continual financial problems and a feeling of failure: '. . . the difficulty in earning my living in a regular fashion despite my reputation, and my taste for the exotic into the bargain made me take an irrevocable decision . . . I am going back to Oceania . . . Nothing will stop me from leaving and it will be forever. What a stupid existence is European life.'[40] This time he intended never to return, 'since my project to bury myself in the Pacific Islands', as he wrote to Maurice Denis.[41] This exile, coupled with his virulent hand in Tahitian political controversy between 1898 and 1899, and the disenchantment born from his work's lack of success, seemed at first to drive him to the role of a simple colonist. 'I am currently organising my life in such a way as to dissociate myself more and more from painting, to withdraw as they say from the art scene by undertaking written work in Tahiti or with a bit of agricultural work on my land.'[42] At this stage, clearly, the dream seemed broken, the man resigned.

Yet there would be a last burst of energy. 'I am grounded today, overwhelmed by misery and especially by the sickness of an altogether premature old age. Will I have some respite so that I can finish my work, I hardly dare to hope: in any case I shall make a last effort next month by moving to live on the still almost cannibalistic Marquesas Island of Fatu Hiva. I believe that there, the entirely savage element, the complete solitude will give me a last fire of enthusiasm before dying which will rejuvenate my imagination and be the conclusion of my talent'[43] (fig.39). In Nerval's words, this really was a yearning for 'a more distant, unattainable Orient'; and an 'Orient' of cannibals, no less, the most savage of 'savages'. Since Tahiti had become a country of colonists, it was necessary to journey further still. To follow this logic – ultimately, the logic of an Orientalist – would be to disappear definitively, to merge with this communion of an 'Orient' at once real and chimerical, visionary and inaccessible. This required a sensitive harmony between the painter and this land of origins, a harmony produced by a certain degree of openness. Such a conclusion was no longer a question of understanding, characterising or clarifying,[44] but of becoming one with the dream, of allowing the landscape and the myth to crystallise in his work. Here the search for a mythical Orient, where man's natural, immemorial links with the world could be restored, finds its terrain. 'The path of the stars and the Desire for the Orient – Europe . . . – the dream becomes real – The seas – memories unravelling through – Men have made me suffer – Climate where my head rests – Loves left in a tomb – She, whom I had lost – . . . – Vessel of the Orient', notes Nerval in his *Carnet du Caire*.[45] On the subject of *Where Do We Come From? What Are We? Where Are We Going?*, Gauguin noted: 'The idol is there not as a literary explanation, but as a statue, less statue perhaps than the animal figures; less animal too, becoming one in my dream, in front of my hut, with the whole of nature, dominating *our primitive soul*, the imaginary consolation of our sufferings and what they contain of the vague and the uncomprehending before the mystery of our origins and our future.'[46] And so that we might bear witness to this dream, so that in Paris his works could be understood as a *veritable* Orient[47] – that is to say, one born of an immaterial, heavenly dream – the painter had to fade, dissolve completely into this timeless – and non-existent – Orient. In some sense, it is as Daniel de Monfreid addressed Gauguin: 'You are currently this extraordinary, legendary artist, who from the depths of Oceania sends disturbing, inimitable works, definitive works of a great man who has in a way disappeared from the world . . . In short, you enjoy the immunity of great dead men, you have passed into the History of Art.'[48] As for Gauguin, he echoed this with a last dream: 'No later than last night I dreamt I was dead and, strangely enough, it was the true instant when I lived happily.'[49]

Translated by Anna Hiddleston and Nancy Ireson

55

GAUGUIN AND SEGALEN: EXOTICISM, MYTH AND THE 'AESTHETICS OF DIVERSITY'

Charles Forsdick

The 'Significant Missed Rendez-Vous'

When, in January 1903, Paul Gauguin's life was drawing to a close, a young French naval doctor thirty years his junior, with literary aspirations and emerging ethnographic interests, arrived in Polynesia. Having recently completed his medical training, Victor Segalen (1878–1919) was entering the first stage of his own short yet intense, diverse and extremely productive career. Segalen's posting as medical officer on the vessel *Durance*, stationed in Papeete but with various duties throughout the French possessions in the Pacific, would be followed throughout the final decade of his life by a number of periods in China. It was such contact with radically different, 'exotic' cultures that would subsequently allow Segalen to become the French author and thinker who most consistently explored questions of cross-cultural encounter, and who also addressed, in the opening decades of the twentieth century, closely associated issues of cultural diversity and its decline.[1]

The anthropologist James Clifford describes the arrival of Segalen on Hiva-Oa in August 1903, three months after Gauguin's death, as a 'significant missed rendez-vous'.[2] Had Segalen, en route for Papeete, not been delayed in San Francisco by the typhoid he contracted whilst crossing the United States, and had his arrival in the Pacific not coincided with a devastating cyclone in the Tuamotu archipelago (to which his ship was called to give emergency aid, and to transport the surviving inhabitants to neighbouring islands), then the two might actually have met. It remains of course a subject of speculation as to how Gauguin would have reacted to the visit of the young naval officer, although Segalen's Breton origins and his association with literary and artistic figures with whom the painter was familiar would undoubtedly have stood him in good stead. In Clifford's view, however, this failure to meet did not serve as an obstacle to Segalen's engagement with Gauguin; it might even be suggested that the lack of direct contact permitted instead a more openly creative, even mythologising interpretation of the artist and of his particular perception of the Pacific.

This interpretation would, in many ways, serve as the foundation of Segalen's struggle during the final fifteen years of his life to articulate what he called an 'Aesthetics of Diversity'. Segalen's exoticism, grounded very clearly in the initial experience of the Pacific, prefigures contemporary, postcolonial debates regarding the globalisation of cultures (and the possibility of resistance to such processes), and has as a result contributed to his growing status as an influential thinker in this field. For Clifford, Segalen serves – along with his near contemporaries Blaise Cendrars (1887–1961) and Antonin Artaud (1896–1948) – as a direct inheritor of Gauguin and Arthur Rimbaud (1854–1891). He is one of a group of writers and artists who challenged the colonial exoticism of the fin-de-siècle as it persisted into the early decades of the twentieth century, and who sought to develop a 'postsymbolist poetics of displacement' dependent on 'more troubling, less stable encounters with the exotic'.[3]

Segalen's contribution to such a poetics is concentrated in a diverse and extensive corpus of works, most of which remained unpublished at his premature death at the age of forty-one. These works reflect his polymathic interests (ranging from ethnography to archaeology, from art history to musicology) as well as his ability

Fig. 40 Daniel de Monfreid
Portrait of Victor Segalen 1909
Oil on canvas
65 x 51
Private Collection

to engage with and often re-engineer a range of literary genres. His oeuvre is customarily divided into a series of 'cycles', reflecting his evolving interests and the changing geo-cultural contexts of his writing.[4] The first of these cycles, after the medico-literary criticism of his very early career, is 'Polynesian' ('le cycle polynésien'), and it is here that Segalen's principal writings on Gauguin are to be found: passages in his travel diary; an early article in the *Mercure de France*; the multiple drafts of an unpublished, semi-biographical novel inspired by the life of the artist; the long introduction to the first edition of Gauguin's letters to Daniel de Monfreid. The apparent neatness of these groupings, however, disguises the fact that Gauguin remained an object of fascination for Segalen throughout his literary career to such an extent that the artist was the subject of both his earliest and his final writings.[5] Gauguin's persistently catalytic role in the evolution of Segalen's thought is equally apparent in his correspondence, in which there are regular references to the artist. His influence is also present in Segalen's Chinese travel journals, where attempts to capture the colour and texture of place rely in a number of cases on references to Gauguin's distinctive gaze and palette.

David Sweetman's characterisation of Segalen as 'the first of many who would build a career out of Gauguin's memory' thus only tells part of the story.[6] Exploring the relationship between Gauguin and Segalen is in fact doubly illuminating: not only does it allow us to understand Segalen's progressive emergence, in this initial Polynesian context, as an artist and thinker, and to explore the ways in which that first contact, in

Fig. 41 *Seated Tahitian* 1896–9
Noa Noa, opening page of Chapter
XII, folio 89 recto, p.171
*Watercolour monotype on wove paper
covered with thin tissue, pasted onto
the manuscript page
Musée du Louvre, Département des
arts graphiques, Fonds Orsay*

Fig. 42 *Max Anély [Victor Segalen]*
Les Immémoriaux
*Paris, Mercure de France, 1907
Limited edition with leather binding
designed by Segalen and executed by
his wife Yvonne
Private Collection*

the work of Gauguin, with a radically different culture (and a radically different way of looking at that culture) constantly shaped his subsequent reflection on exoticism, most notably in China; but it also permits us to track key stages in the rapid emergence of Gauguin's own afterlife as an increasingly fictionalised and mythologised figure of more generally symbolic proportions.

'He was called Paul Gauguin'

In a letter to his parents from the Marquesas Islands, dated 5 August 1903, Segalen recounts his medical duties among the indigenous population: 'seventy-five children vaccinated, sixty-five teeth extracted'. He goes on to outline the way he was spending his free time: 'On a neighbouring island, a painter who had escaped from the Symbolist school has just died . . . I have enjoyed piously going through his manuscripts, collecting impressions of his final days that I am going to send to his friends in Paris who will be grateful to me for having defended, from so far away, a group to which I am increasingly attracted. He was called Paul Gauguin.'[7] Despite the nonchalant tone of the correspondence and the implication that his family were unfamiliar with the painter, Segalen himself was certainly aware of Gauguin's work before his departure for the Pacific, not least because of his contact with figures in the Symbolist and post-Symbolist milieu of the *Mercure de France*, including Remy de Gourmont (1858–1915) and Saint-Pol-Roux (1861–1940). He was also acquainted with Dr Gouzer, a naval doctor like himself, who had been one of Segalen's supervisors at the hospital in Brest during his studies there in 1898. Gouzer had met Gauguin in 1897, during his own tour of duty in the Pacific, and appears to have bought a canvas from the painter (possibly it was a gift, according to de Monfreid), which it is likely that Segalen had seen before his departure from France in 1902.[8]

As Segalen's later 'Hommage à Gauguin' (1918) makes clear, the preliminary information he received in the field was less sympathetic, with one interlocutor responding to enquiries in a particularly dismissive manner: 'Gauguin? A mad man. He painted pink horses.'[9] Segalen remained curious, however, about this compatriot living remotely on Hiva-Oa, around nine hundred miles from Tahiti and about a week away from the Polynesian capital by sea. There is no evidence that he was at this time aware either of Gauguin's legal difficulties or of the trial he underwent shortly before his death for defamation of a government official (he was fined 500 francs and sentenced to three months' imprisonment), and when the painter died on 8 May 1903 Segalen was in New Caledonia, only receiving the news of his death on his return to Tahiti in early June. By a happy coincidence, however, it was the *Durance* that was sent to the Marquesas Islands to collect Gauguin's remaining possessions. Segalen's ship arrived at Nuku-Hiva, the archipelago's administrative capital, on 3 August, and it was there that the young medical officer had his initial contact with what he dubbed in his diary 'traces' of the painter. In the local administrator's house, Segalen was able to sift through a case of manuscripts, letters and other papers taken from the dwelling on Hiva-Oa. As the remainder of Gauguin's possessions not already sold at auction in the artist's 'House of Pleasure' on 20 July were transported to Papeete for a second sale, it was these 'relics' that he consulted on board ship, transcribing several passages into his *Journal des îles*.

Segalen compensated for the absence left by Gauguin's death by attempting to recover whatever traces of him were left. He talked to the artist's friends, spoke to those such as Tioka and Ky Dong who had been with him in his final months, and met local figures including the gendarme Jean-Pierre Claverie and the Protestant missionary Paul Vernier, both of whom had played key roles in the circumstances surrounding Gauguin's death. Segalen also visited the 'House of Pleasure' itself while on Hiva-Oa, using his observations and interviews to reconstruct – in a way that David Sweetman accurately sees as 'more fanciful that factual' – an account of the artist's final days.[10] Unusually, Segalen's initial direct contact with Gauguin's life and work was therefore not so much through his painting as through his writing and thought. Thirteen manuscripts were included in the chests transported on the *Durance*,[11] and Segalen's

Fig.43 Breton Village in the Snow 1894
Oil on canvas
62 x 87
Musée d'Orsay, Paris

diary contains transcribed passages from the artist's expanded and annotated edition of *Noa-Noa* (fig.41) as well as from the then unpublished *Cahier pour Aline*, of which he was almost certainly the first reader (no.126).[12] These texts by Gauguin clearly had a direct influence on Segalen's own Polynesian writings (and on the substantial correspondence he wrote while in the region), in which there are very clear traces of the artist's reflections on the devastating effects of colonial contact, on the aesthetics of representing the Pacific and its peoples, and on the affective dimensions of his personal contact with Polynesian culture. Gauguin's manuscripts can also be seen as a clear inspiration for, or at least galvanisation of, Segalen's plans for his first major work, the ethnographic novel *Les Immémoriaux*, which would appear in 1907 (fig.42).[13] The impact of this encounter with Gauguin's work would persist throughout the remainder of Segalen's life, with the artist embodying the more general intellectual, aesthetic and deeply personal impact that Segalen's stay in Polynesia itself had generated.

Papeete, 2 September 1903

On his return to Papeete on 20 August 1903, Segalen was involved in what has become one of the key scenes in modern accounts of exoticism in the French-speaking world (as well as one of the most regrettable episodes in the history of modern art): the auction of the fifteen cases of Gauguin's remaining possessions that had arrived back in Tahiti the same day. Segalen had already had the opportunity to examine closely these artefacts on board the *Durance*, and the experience had clearly strengthened his resolve to invest the equivalent of almost a month's salary in purchasing twenty-four lots in the sale on 2 September.[14] Already aware, from his observations on Hiva-Oa, of the misunderstanding to which Gauguin's work was widely subject, Segalen's reaction to the auction may be read as an act of salvage that represents at the same time a seminal moment in the construction of Gauguin's posthumous reputation. The local authorities had discarded a number of lots judged unfit for sale, and the keenest interest was in Gauguin's carriage, furniture and other household possessions. The attitude to his art was principally one of derision. As Gilles Manceron notes, this public response is reflected in the fact that the artist's sewing machine was sold for eighty francs, whereas one of his canvases went for a mere two francs.[15] Segalen records that when the canvas of *Breton Village in the Snow* (fig.43), which he subsequently purchased, was held up on its side, the auctioneer dismissed it as an image of Niagara Falls, much to the amusement of the crowd.[16]

*Fig.44 Self-portrait near
Golgotha 1896
Oil on canvas
76 x 64
Museu de Arte, São Paolo*

For Segalen, who by this stage had already assumed the role of the artist's 'inflexible champion', purchasing Gauguin's relics was an 'act of piety' and an element of what he saw as 'fighting the good fight' against the philistine religious and colonial authorities.[17] Of extremely limited means, Segalen nevertheless managed to secure seven of the ten canvases included in the sale, as well as a large number of prints, photographs, drawings, books, sketchbooks and carvings (including, most significantly, the panels that had surrounded the door of the 'House of Pleasure' (no.155).[18] Much of the remaining material was either scattered or discarded, but Segalen is to be credited with saving key works such as *Scene of Tahitian Life* and *Self-portrait near Golgotha* – one of Gauguin's final paintings in which he depicts himself – a canvas in such poor condition that he had it restored on his return to France (fig.44). In addition to two other unidentified paintings, he also purchased a second Breton canvas, *Christmas Night* (fig.51), described in his diary among the objects initially discovered at Nuku-Hiva. Among the lots Segalen acquired was a further key relic that he would subsequently use to suggest that *Breton Village in the Snow* had been the artist's final work, namely, Gauguin's palette, purchased for a derisory two francs.

Segalen undoubtedly saw the purchase of such a range of lots as an automatic means of gaining an entrée to those artistic circles in Paris in which, on his return to France, he aspired to move. It was certainly a crucial act of protection, in a material sense and in terms both of Gauguin's and his own reputation, that would win him favour with members of the artist's circle, such as George-Daniel de Monfreid, who he met in 1905 and with whom he indeed developed a close association. De Monfreid painted what is perhaps the best-known portrait of Segalen in 1909 (fig.40), which shows the author seated at his desk beside Gauguin's sculpture, the *Idol with a Pearl*, and painting, *La Barque* (no.85). At the same time, however, Segalen's purchases reflect the impulsive and instinctive reaction that the indirect encounter with Gauguin triggered in him, a response that he described toward the end of his life, in 'Hommage à Gauguin', in terms of a 'duty'.[19] The objects that he brought back with him to France were slowly dispersed (a process continued after his death by his family), both as gifts and, with the steady rise of Gauguin's reputation, as a source of income; and these artefacts continued to be subject to journeys of their own. The carvings from the 'House of Pleasure' were, for instance, lent to Saint-Pol-Roux in 1905 to decorate his home on the Crozon Peninsula in Brittany, until Segalen requested their return during the First World War when he sought inspiration for his text 'Hommage à Gauguin'; they remained in the family, featuring in a photograph that accompanied an article about Segalen's daughter published in *Vogue*, before being acquired – along with canvases and other items – by the Louvre in 1952.

'Gauguin in his final setting'

In his *Journal des îles* Segalen transcribed the final line of Gauguin's *Cahier pour Aline*: 'To my daughter Aline, scattered notes, discontinuous like Dreams, like Life made up entirely of different pieces.'[20] The fragmentation described here reflects equally the material – both concrete artefacts and gathered information – with which Segalen himself was left after both the visit to the Marquesas and the auction at Papeete. It was nevertheless from such sources that Segalen began to assemble the multifaceted image of Gauguin to whose construction he would continue to contribute until his own premature death in 1919. For David Sweetman, the privileged yet indirect access to the material sites and artefacts associated with the end of Gauguin's life triggered, almost immediately after the artist's death, the processes of his mythologisation: 'Segalen was a worthy disciple in the way that his account of Gauguin's life in Atuona merges truth and fiction, launching the myth of the solitary artist-hero of the Pacific, the tortured genius.'[21] Segalen was a key figure in the posthumous recognition of Gauguin, not only because of the salvage of works and other relics at the auction on 2 September 1903, but also because he would go on to publish the first detailed account of Gauguin's final weeks and of his physical surroundings at the time of his death.

Segalen wrote letters to a number of Gauguin's key friends and associates – Charles Morice, Saint-Pol-Roux, Remy de Gourmont and Daniel de Monfreid –

Fig.45 Self-portrait drawing
c.1902–3
Pencil on paper
15 x 10
Musée du Louvre, Département
des arts graphiques, Fonds Orsay

to inform them of the painter's death, but it was in 'Gauguin dans son dernier décor' ('Gauguin in his final setting'), which appeared in the *Mercure de France* in June 1904, that we read his first published reflections on his visit to Hiva-Oa. The article retains an immediacy and freshness that result in part from the fact that Segalen, despite his failure to meet Gauguin, was one of only a few observers sympathetic to the artist to be in the Pacific at around the time of his death. The text presents the (reconstructed) surroundings of the artist in his final days in theatrical terms, and describes the objects left in his dwelling in the terms of quasi-religious relics. Among these, he focuses in particular on works he purchased at the auction – most notably *Self-portrait near Golgotha* and sculpted panels that had been placed around the door of Gauguin's 'House of Pleasure' (four of the five of which he had purchased at auction). In a reference to *Breton Village in the Snow*, Segalen also for the first time makes the apocryphal claim – repeated elsewhere in his work – that, shortly before Gauguin's death, the artist had focused on the radically different vision of a snow-covered Brittany.[22]

Central to the article is an attempt to encapsulate Gauguin's outsider and even 'outlaw' status, and this study is the likely foundation of Segalen's later unfinished project, entitled *Les Hors-la-Loi* (Outlaws), in which the artist was to have figured alongside other figures such as Rimbaud. The reference to *Near Golgotha* alludes also to the artist's own conscious self-fashioning, and it is significant that among the lots purchased by Segalen was an additional undated sketch, *Self-portrait drawing*, for which he paid fifteen francs (fig.45). Adopting a stance reminiscent of Auguste Rodin's (1840–1917) *The Thinker*, Gauguin shows himself as fragile, emaciated and deep in thought. As a result of observing these works, Segalen becomes aware from an early stage of the artist's self-performative, self-mythologising tendencies, and the efforts to project a certain version of himself that this betokens. Segalen actively contributed to these efforts by laying the foundations for Gauguin's posthumous mythologisation, and 'Gauguin dans son dernier décor' ends with the particularly enigmatic phrase of the artist's companion Tioka: 'Now there are no more men.'[23] By recording this mournful observation, Segalen signals the sense that Gauguin's death constitutes the premature conclusion of an aesthetic project similar to his own, the aim of which was to capture traces of a culture in decline before its distinctiveness was lost to the entropic effects of colonialism and Westernisation.

Mythologising Gauguin: The Master-of-Pleasure

'Gauguin dans son dernier décor' was Segalen's first published literary work. With it – fifteen years before Somerset Maugham had published *The Moon and Sixpence*, his 1919 short novel inspired by Gauguin's life, and almost a century in advance of Mario Vargas Llosa's *The Way to Paradise* (2003) – he began the processes of fictionalising Gauguin's life that have played a central role in the more general mythologisation to which he has been subject. Segalen himself worked for almost a decade, between 1907 and 1916, on a fictional account of Gauguin's life entitled *Le Maître-du-Jouir* (The Master-of-Pleasure), the final manuscript of which he had hoped to complete during a six-month stay in the Pacific after the First World War. The novel constitutes a clear shift from history to myth, and Segalen outlines the project in a letter to the philosopher and essayist Jules de Gaultier, where he describes his protagonist, a semi-prophetic Western character with Nietzschean overtones, whose aim is to re-infuse Tahitian culture with what it has lost, 'joyous, naked life'. He continues: 'The painter Gauguin sketched out, with certain aspects of his life, the outline of this man. It is a matter of re-imagining his dream.'[24] The published version of the novel begins with a statement of ignorance: 'I did not know this man, or at least not his living person, and I do not claim ever to have got close to him.' But this distance permits the emergence in the text of a re-imagined, mythologised figure whom Segalen describes as feeling a growing anxiety regarding the Western presence in the Pacific and the apparent indifference of the indigenous population to the implications of that presence. The planned novel begins where Segalen's *Les Immémoriaux* concludes. It outlines the efforts of the eponymous hero to recover 'dead voices' and to counter an aesthetics of cultural decline (associated in Segalen's mind with the exoticist fictions of Pierre Loti in particular) by adopting a

Fig. 46 *Portrait of Victor Segalen*
1904
Photograph
14 x 9.8
Private Collection

subversive, regenerative form of artistic intervention that permits a new generation of Tahitians to unlearn Western teaching and influence, to rediscover and reconnect with traditions seen as forgotten or lost.

Segalen presents the artist's project as a form of external intervention to protect Pacific cultures against not only European influence but also indigenous indifference to that influence. Recent scholars have often countered the interpretation of Gauguin represented in *Le Maître-du-Jouir*, a text that is characterised equally by a violent reaction against all manifestations of cultural and biological hybridity. Some have seen in Gauguin an attempt to capture a culture in transition, in which the indigenous and the Western are juxtaposed and seen in a process of negotiating the relationships that connect them; others have signalled the artist's denial of local agency, and his inability to imagine an indigenous response to the nefarious effects of cultural contact. In relation to the latter, Stephen F. Eisenman claims: 'For Victor Segalen, Gauguin was every bit as racially exotic a being as the Marquesans with whom he lived; his works and personal effects must therefore be gathered together before they turned to dust, before that is, they joined the forgotten memories ('les immémoriaux') of the Polynesians themselves. Like Gauguin, however, the native people of the Pacific refused to become relics and pass into the tomb of history.'[25]

Such a postcolonial interpretation may be seen to detect the ideological blind spots in both Gauguin and Segalen, but there is a risk that such retrospective interpretations ignore the divergence between the aesthetics of diversity on which their work depends and the received wisdom regarding other people and cultures evident in the cultural production of the majority of their contemporaries. Segalen, like Gauguin, was the product of a particular historical niche, and the author discovered in the work of the artist a means of critiquing the context from which he emerged. The impact of Gauguin on Segalen's work was not restricted to his Polynesian texts: it is in evidence throughout the reflection on exoticism that would dominate Segalen's career. Perhaps his key work is the unfinished, undoubtedly unfinishable *Essai sur l'exotisme* (Essay on Exoticism), an accumulation of fragments produced over fourteen years between 1904 and 1918. The role of Gauguin in this work is evident from the outset: in the opening note – drafted off Java in October 1904, as Segalen returned home to Brittany from his first tour of duty – the impact of Polynesia is underlined, and the centrality of the artist is apparent from his inclusion in a list relating to painting and exoticism.

The only other reference to Gauguin relates to Segalen's supposition – subsequently challenged by scholars, as has been discussed above – that the final work on which Gauguin had worked whilst on Hiva-Oa was *Breton Village in the Snow*, the canvas of which he claimed had been found on its easel at Gauguin's death. Segalen's own relationship to his native Brittany was a contradictory one, characterised not only by the chronic extroversion that motivated his endless travelling, but also a complementary attraction that constantly drew him back to the region where he himself would die prematurely in May 1919. The image of the dying artist ignoring his tropical Marquesan surroundings and longing for the Breton winter thus appealed doubly to Segalen, as a reflection of his own ambivalent relationship toward the region, but also as an example of the radical alternation between differences on which his concept of exoticism depends. Segalenian exoticism may be seen to evolve according to two stages. The initial phase, inspired by the author's experiences in the Pacific, suggests that exoticism is in fact bilateral and not simply ethnocentric, and permits as a result a reversal of perspective according to which the Western traveller is viewed through non-Western eyes, being subsequently exoticised. The second stage, associated with Segalen's contact with China, focuses instead on the opacity or radical alterity of cultures, and their potential resistance to an external gaze. The impact of Gauguin is apparent in each of these stages, for despite their different emphases both depend on diverse senses as a mode of mediating otherness, both imply a reciprocity as a result of which the stability of Western travellers' identities is itself challenged by the presence of those they meet. As Segalen outlines in 'Hommage à Gauguin', what he principally discovered in Gauguin was an alternative way of seeing: 'Before him . . . no convincing image of a Maori had been seen in Europe . . . From now on, no traveller can claim to have fully seen the landscape and inhabitants of these islands if they have not been revealed and explained to him through Gauguin's canvases.'[26] The impact of Gauguin's aesthetics on his own approach to writing became apparent early, for as he wrote to de Monfreid in 1906, in relation to *Les Immémoriaux*: 'I have tried to "write" the Tahitians in a manner similar to the way in which Gauguin saw them to paint them: in themselves and from inside outwards.'[27]

The 'significant missed rendez-vous' of 1903 had such an impact on Segalen that he spent the next fifteen years of his life attempting to understand who Gauguin was and what, posthumously, he meant for Western art and its representation of other cultures. Segalen's notion of exoticism is the outcome of such a reflection, and from the artist this concept draws a number of questions that continue to influence those who explore cultural difference and the modes of its representation. To what extent does Western art attempt to tame non-Western cultures, or to what extent might those cultures generate instead a troubling inverse exoticism, destabilising accordingly established aesthetic assumptions and practices? How might the alternation or contrast of cultural extremes disrupt the emergence of an entropic middle ground associated with levelling forces such as, in a contemporary context, globalisation? And, finally, might the role of the creative artist be not the domestication of other cultures but rather the representation of their persistent opacity, their ultimate impenetrability when faced with an intrusive external gaze?

GAUGUIN: A VERY BRITISH RECEPTION

Amy Dickson

Fig.47 *Poster for 'Manet and the Post-Impressionists' at the Grafton Galleries* 1910

A century has passed since Roger Fry's groundbreaking exhibition *Manet and the Post-Impressionists* opened at the Grafton Galleries in London with a private view on the evening of 5 November 1910. The impact of the exhibition was immediate and explosive, with over fifty articles appearing in the press in November alone.[1] In a letter to his father, Fry described the 'wild hurricane of newspaper abuse from all quarters'.[2] Criticism ranged from the comical to the sinister: H.M. Bateman's humorous cartoon for the *Bystander*, 'Post-Impressions of the Post-Impressionists', depicts an English gentleman in top hat and tails, upright and respectable 'before' his trip to the Grafton Galleries, then bent over, swooning, mopping his brow 'after' the experience, as well as caricatures of the well-to-do clutching their sides and each other in uncontrollable mirth at the sight of this new art (fig.48). Robert Ross's wry review in the *Morning Post* was explicit in its political implication: 'A date more favourable than the Fifth of November for revealing the existence of a wide-spread plot to destroy the whole fabric of European painting could hardly have been chosen.'[3] Ross's review itself was critical dynamite when considered against the backdrop of contemporary concerns about social and political unrest, from the constant news reports about anarchist groups active in Europe to the mobilisation of the suffragette movement, which by 1910 was gaining momentum at home.

The 1910 exhibition, which was visited by around 25,000 people during its run of two months, proved a *succès de scandale*, playing a significant role in bringing 'modern art' into the British consciousness and in the development of a critical discourse around 'modernism'. Fry's selection of works for the show was decidedly influenced by Julius Meier-Graefe's seminal book, *Modern Art: Being a Contribution to a New System of Aesthetics* (1904), recently translated into English (1908).[4] Three of Meier-Graefe's modernist protagonists, Paul Cézanne, Vincent Van Gogh and Paul Gauguin, emerged through the 1910 show into the collective British mind as pioneers of modern art. With more works in the show than the other artists, and his *Poèmes Barbares* of 1896 as the poster image for the exhibition (fig.47), Gauguin's prominence was noted by the British artist Spencer Gore (1878–1914): 'Of all the painters represented here Gauguin seems to be the least disliked. He is certainly the best represented.'[5] Thirty-seven Gauguins were hung in two main groups in the Large Gallery and the Centre Gallery. Tahitian works including the controversial yet popular *Manao tupapau* (no.121) dominated the former, and Breton works including *Christ in the Garden of Olives* (no.9) dominated the latter.[6] Other smaller groups of works featured elsewhere in the exhibition.[7]

An unsigned review from the *Daily Express*, 9 November 1910, 'Paint Run Mad', demonstrates the overwhelming emphasis on 'primitivism' in the contemporary British discourse around Gauguin's work: 'In the large gallery the eye meets Gauguin's primitive, almost barbaric, studies of Tahitian women – bizarre, morbid and horrible.'[8] As scholar Bullen has commented, such responses were 'coloured by a number of contradictory prejudices, preconceptions and received ideas, many of which were socially, culturally, aesthetically and even scientifically determined'.[9] These contradictions allowed critics to pen 'lurid accounts aimed both to repel and titillate'; and framed in this way, Gauguin's works would undoubtedly have had anthropological appeal for a British public whose understanding of Polynesian culture was largely limited

Fig. 48 Cartoon from 'Bystander'
23 November 1910
Private Collection

FOSTED, NEAR THE GRAFTON GALLERIES, BY H. M. BATEMAN

to ethnographic displays and museum cabinets of curiosities.[10] Furthermore, 'the term [primitive] is used to evoke. It is never clearly defined. "Primitive" aspects of Gauguin's life and the "primitive" style he evolved in response to "primitive" subjects are interchangeable.' This slippage between Gauguin as 'primitive' and the 'primitivism' in his oeuvre is symptomatic of the conflation of his life and work in contemporary critical responses, which focussed on his unconventional lifestyle and intriguing biography, romanticising it as indicative of his artistic genius.[11] Indeed, C. Lewis Hind described him as 'the "great barbarian" who fled from Europe and civilisation, painted the walls of mudhuts in Tahiti, and died on one of the islands',[12] and Laurence Binyon hinted at the importance placed on biography conflated with notions of 'genius' in his statement, 'you feel the interest of a personality behind the work'.[13]

It is unsurprising that the myth of Gauguin as the artist-genius-gone-native dominated British contemporary critical discourse in the year 1910–11: Meier-Graefe's influential account of Gauguin in *Modern Art*, the first scholarly account of the new movement, is firmly rooted in a heroic reading of the artist's biography and particularly his South Sea odyssey, as recounted in *Noa Noa*. The latter had been published by unquestionably address certain Jewish stereotypes, these images should not lightly be given such a negative interpretation. Certainly Gauguin was intrigued by de Haan's absorption with his Jewish identity – which presumably manifested itself in his conversation as well as in his dress and sombre demeanour. Allowance should also be made for de Haan's own agency. For it was only through him that Gauguin had any sort of access to Carlyle's book, *Sartor Resartus*, whose eccentric central character, Professor Teufelsdrökh, offers an obvious and humorous literary pretext for Gauguin's playing with the melancholic or devilish aspects of his friend. Interestingly, if Carlyle and Milton became an increasing preoccupation for Gauguin from this date on, so did Rembrandt. What is unclear is whether de Haan himself retained any of Gauguin's images.[15]

This sequence of images coincided with the artists' protracted period working and living together in Le Pouldu, a more successful and harmonious reprise, from Gauguin's point of view, of his cohabitation with Vincent van Gogh. Gauguin's mentoring role, his admiration for de Haan's talent and the generally bantering humour that characterised the artistic community of Brittany all played a part in the relationship. There was no open animosity between them, de Haan expressing his profound admiration for Gauguin in a letter to Theo. Just at the time of their supposed rivalry for the favours of Marie Henry, they were planning to make the trip together to Tahiti.[16] Gauguin later wrote to his wife Mette regretting de Haan's decision not to come, and complaining of the solitude that he was enduring as a result.[17]

Although he was well aware of de Haan's fragile health, it is not known whether Gauguin learned of his friend's early death in 1895. If he did know of it, it might explain de Haan's mask-like features resurfacing in a woodcut datable to 1896–7 and in two later paintings. In the woodcut, the same configuration of the earlier melancholic face-in-hand motif floats before a gaunt spectre and a dark-haired, possibly Tahitian, woman in three-quarter view (no.12). De Haan's features hover, like a memory, behind a floral still life of uncertain date.[9] Finally, his crouching persona, clad in a blue dress, the *vahine*'s voluminous missionary-style smock, but revealing devilish clawed feet, makes a last surreal appearance in the extraordinarily powerful but wilfully enigmatic composition *Contes barbares* of 1902 (no.154).

Fig.55 <u>Portrait of Meijer de Haan</u> 1889–90
Gouache on cotton
20 x 29
Wadsworth Atheneum Museum of Art,
Hartford. The Ella Gallup Sumner and
Mary Catlin Sumner Collection Fund

2
Self-Portrait c.1876
Oil on canvas
46.7 x 38.4
Harvard Art Museum / Fogg Museum,
Cambridge, MA. Gift of Helen W.
Ellsworth in memory of Duncan S.
Ellsworth '22, nephew of Archibald
A. Hutchinson, benefactor of the
Hutchinson Wing

3
Self-Portrait with Palette c.1893–4
Oil on canvas
92 x 73
Private Collection

4
Embellished Frame or Frame with Two
Interlaced 'G's 1881–3
Carved walnut containing a photograph
of the artist (photograph c.1885)
18.9 x 33.6 x 1
Musée d'Orsay, Paris. Gift of Corinne
Peterson, in memory of Fredrick
Peterson and Lucy Peterson, 2003

5
Self-Portrait Vase in the Form of a
Severed Head 1889
Stoneware
h.19.5
The Danish Museum of Art & Design,
Copenhagen

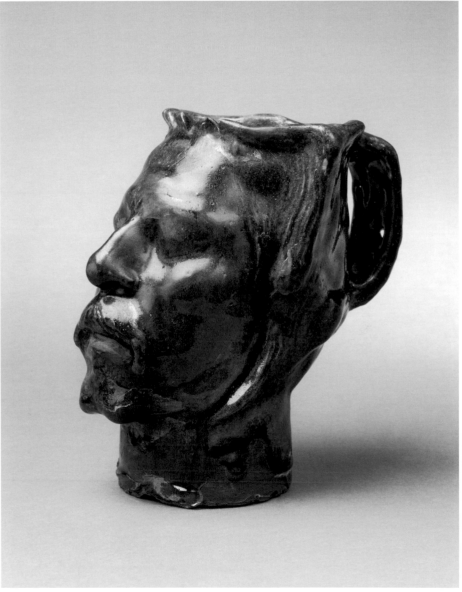

17
Self-Portrait with Manao tupapau 1893–4
Oil on canvas
46 x 38
Musée d'Orsay, Paris

18
Self-Portrait with Portraits of Roderic
O'Conor and Jacob Meijer de Haan 1890
Crayon on paper
28.8 x 45
The J.F. Willumsen Museum, Frederikssund
Denmark

19
Tahitians: Sheet of studies with six heads 1894
Colour monotype printed on paper
24 x 20
The Trustees of the British Museum, London

20
Headpiece for 'Le Sourire' 1899–1900
Woodcut printed on paper, above
drawing in watercolour, pen and ink and
crayon; sheet laid down on board
29.6 x 20.4
The Art Institute of Chicago. Gift of
Walter S. Brewster

89

26
Inside the Painter's House, rue Carcel 1881
Oil on canvas
103.5 x 162.5
Nasjonalmuseet for kunst, arkitektur og
design, Oslo

27
Still Life with Peonies 1884
Oil on canvas
59.7 x 73
National Gallery of Art, Washington.
Collection of Mr and Mrs Paul Mellon

28
Still Life with Sunflowers on an Armchair
1901
Oil on canvas
66 x 75.5
Bührle Foundation, Zurich

29
Still Life with Sketch by Delacroix 1887
Oil on canvas
45 x 30
Musée d'Art moderne et contemporain de
Strasbourg

'I am doing some art pottery. Schuff says they are masterpieces, so does the maker, but they are probably too artistic to be sold. However given time ... perhaps ... they will be an amazing success. I hope the Devil is listening!'
Letter to Mette, 26 December 1886

'If you are curious to see all the little products of my crazy ideas (hautes folies) now that they've come out of the kiln, they're ready – 55 pieces in good condition. You are bound to cry out in horror at these monstrosities but I am convinced they will interest you.'
Letter to Félix Bracquemond, late 1886 or early 1887

30
<u>*Double Vessel with Mask of Woman*</u>
1887–8
Glazed and unglazed stoneware with touches of gold
h.19.5
Ny Carlsberg Glyptotek, Copenhagen

31
<u>*Still Life with Profile of Laval*</u> *1886*
Oil on canvas
46 x 38.1
Indianapolis Museum of Art. Samuel Josefowitz Collection of the School of Pont-Avon, through the generosity of Lilly Endowment Inc., the Josefowitz Family, Mr and Mrs James M. Cornelius, Mr and Mrs Leonard J. Betley, Lori and Dan Efroymson, and other Friends of the Museum

32
Two Children c.1889
Oil on canvas
46 x 60
Ny Carlsberg Glyptotek, Copenhagen

33
Still Life with Fruit 1888
Oil on canvas
43 x 58
The State Pushkin Museum of Fine
Arts, Moscow

34
Still Life with Three Puppies 1888
Oil on wood
91.8 x 62.6
The Museum of Modern Art, New York.
Mrs Simon Guggenheim Fund, 1952

LANDSCAPE
AND RURAL
NARRATIVE

*You're a Parisianist. Give me the country. I love Brittany: I find the
wild and the primitive here. When my clogs resonate on this granite
ground I hear the muffled and powerful thud that I'm looking for
in painting. All that is very sad ... but to each painter his character.*[1]

*I am trying to put into these desolate figures the savagery
that I see in them and which is in me too ... Dammit, I want to
consult nature as well but I don't want to leave out what I see there
and what comes into my mind.*[2]

Gauguin to Émile Schuffenecker and Vincent van Gogh

Fig.58 <u>Blue Trees</u> or *'Vous y
passerez, la belle'* 1888
Oil on canvas
92 x 73
Ordrupgaard, Copenhagen

111

For all his antipathy to what he calls 'Parisianism', Gauguin was
by no means a natural countryman. It took him some time to
devise strategies for representing the rural life and landscape
of Brittany, Martinique or Oceania in ways that captured his
fascination with their difference and registered his own presence.
When working in a new place, unlike other contemporary
artists, Gauguin steered clear of sites of dramatic topographical
or architectural interest in favour of more intimate habitats that
revealed the indigenous population. Building on his apprenticeship
with Camille Pissarro, which had equipped him for dealing with
the characteristics of vegetation without becoming lost or unduly
detained, he sought a way to unlock the essence of a place through
figure drawing. In every new setting he concentrated, in sketch
after sketch, on studying the typical physiognomy of the local
inhabitants, how body shape and gestural language were dictated
by different styles of dress, and on observing the rapport between
figures and nature. Inspired by the experience of unfamiliarity
that drove him to ever more extreme shores, Gauguin sought to
instil an equivalence to that excitement of 'dépaysement', of his
intrusiveness as an alien even, into his representations. In a sense
he was performing a balancing act between trying to surrender
to another set of cultural norms and asserting his own identity
and cultural expectations.

Gauguin's approach has been much trumpeted as
primitivising – not least by himself – in its desire to attack what
he saw as the corrupt and decadent aesthetic of the West by
asserting the values of strength, simplicity, crudeness and purity
that he found in non-Western art forms. In this respect his work
is heir to broader nostalgic and reactionary tendencies in
nineteenth-century art such as one finds in Romanticism and
Orientalism. But running counter to Gauguin's conscious desire
for simplification – and disdain for the modern – was the narrative
complication. In 1887 in his first tropical landscapes with figures,
Among the Mangos (fig.19), *Women in a Mango Grove* (no.42) and
Comings and Goings, Martinique (no.45), he set out to represent
the gestures and activities that were assumed to embody the
essential character of the Antillaise 'négresse'. Folkish superstition
was enshrined in the landscape of Brittany too, where every
prominent feature – especially rocks and springs thought to have
spiritual or magical properties – had a local name. But Gauguin
avoided the documentary recording of such features, his whole
approach seeking rather to elicit the special consonance of figure
and field, actor and setting. In his early paintings and ceramics

Fig.59 Among the Lilies 1889
Oil on canvas
92.5 x 73.5
Hilti Art Foundation, Liechtenstein

Gauguin openly embraced popular clichés. He played, for example, to the humorous but patronising analogies drawn by contemporary writers and caricaturists between *Bretonne* and goose (no.50) or *Bretonne* and cow (no.57).

Another narrative strategy was to give an otherwise neutral rural scene a loaded, perplexing title, drawing attention to figural activity that might otherwise pass unnoticed. In the case of three works from Arles, which Gauguin sent in 1889 to the important independent avant-garde exhibition of 'Les XX', he substituted titles clearly meant to pique the viewer's curiosity for the more straightforward ones he had first noted in a sketchbook – *Les Cochons* becoming *En Pleine Chaleur*, *Vendanges à Arles* becoming *Misères humaines*. In the case of one landscape (previously and subsequently known as *Blue Trees*), the sexual innuendo of the title '*Vous y passerez, la belle!*' strayed so far from the ostensible motif that it has only been possible to reconnect the two from a careful reading of the critics (fig.58).[3] Elsewhere one finds instances of what one might call truncated narratives. The intrusion of the outsized hound in *Among the Lilies*, and the strangely prominent red dog in *Harvest: Le Pouldu* (no.54) – in both cases literally imported from a painting by Gustave Courbet formerly owned by Arosa (fig.11) – hints that all is not as it might seem. Furthermore, as a symbol of perversity or as an alter ego, the fox image reached a peak of potency in two overtly symbolic works, *Soyez amoureuses* (no.93) and *The Loss of Virginity* (no.55). But it is instructive to compare the success of the latter with a painting in which that poetic ambiguity tipped over, producing something more akin to melodrama, *Pont-Aven, Village Drama* (fig.60).

Animal imagery offered Gauguin a conveniently ambiguous secondary level of meaning that he would sustain in Polynesia, where he was delighted, for instance, to learn that the ubiquitous pigs had been introduced by missionaries as a substitute for human flesh (nos.58, 60). Just as Gauguin the draughtsman sought to isolate essential differences of contour, gait and body language, Gauguin the musician was alert to differences of sound and language whose understanding was initially closed to him – his clogs on granite, for instance, or a phrase like 'Haere mae', which he frequently heard called out by Tahitian women, only later discovering it meant 'Come eat'. Although the analogy he frequently made between colour harmonies and music is widely

with Breton motifs he gave the scenes a quaintly picture-book look, assigning the lead roles to children as in *The Breton Shepherdess* (no.43) and *Breton Girls Dancing, Pont-Aven* (no.48); increasingly, he lent them an inexplicably wistful demeanour, in works such as *En Bretagne* (no.52) and *Among the Lilies* (fig.59). This sadness, with which he also infused his Breton religious paintings, was characteristic, so he claimed, both of the locale and of his own personality (no.51). And in paintings and prints where he made Martiniquaises or Bretonnes the main subject (largely ignoring the male population, as has often been remarked), acknowledged and respected, little interest has been shown in his recourse to words and language or the uses to which he put aural stimuli.[4] The fragments of overheard foreign conversation that he inscribed onto paintings were a facet, with folklore and myth, of his attempt to play on cultural difference, his search for an essential otherness, drawing attention to his own presence as the foreigner.

In Brittany, Gauguin forced a marriage between his vision of the region, whose lines and colours he deliberately exaggerated and simplified, and the local objects of religious cult, in order to produce a charged spirituality. In Tahiti, he hoped to achieve a similar conjunction of luxuriant setting and eloquent indigenous artefact. On arrival in Papeete in June 1891, however, he soon realised that the Tahitian landscape had been cleaned out of its old icons, and if he wanted it to have a mystic, spiritual dimension, he would have to supply it. The sort of thing Gauguin might have hoped to find was anticipated in a description by Pierre Loti of travelling up to a remote temple in the mountains of Japan and finding strange threatening deities set into rocks or on promontaries, granitic carvings overgrown by foliage; in his poetic evocation of this arcane world, Loti conflated the reality of the Japanese landscape with reminiscences of Tahiti, 'l'île délicieuse', and Brittany, whose familiar church spires, crosses and calvaries he sought in vain. If Gauguin read this text, it could only have fired his project of resurrecting Oceania's lost domains.[5]

After a year or so assembling 'documents', Gauguin began to confect, alongside his more straightforward depictions, Tahitian landscapes and rural scenes that satisfied his imaginings, fusing the possible with the impossible according to his 'dream'. Often he did this by introducing into his paintings a seemingly natural standing 'tiki' (no.73) or larger idol (no.76), inspired by one of his own carvings. Emboldened by his readings in Jacques-Antoine Moerenhout's ethnographic account *Voyage aux îles du grand océan* (1837), he had started the process of devising appropriate forms for the Polynesian theogony, first in rubbings and watercolour illustrations. He drew one of his first tikis in a letter to his wife Mette in the spring of 1892 (no.74). The presence of this or a similar carved idol in the background of certain key 1892 paintings, *Mata Mua* (*In Olden Times*) for instance (no.63), and *Parahi te Marae* (*There Lies the Temple*) (no.87), brings a narrative dimension to these lyrical landscapes, and such idols crop up more overtly in the background of figure compositions

with landscape settings such as *Vairaumati tei oa* (*Her Name is Vairaumati*), *Arearea no Varua ino* (*Words of the Devil*) (nos. 79, 80) or *Mahana no Atua* (*Day of God*) (no.81). As in the previous decade, this fusion of personal, charged, three-dimensional crafted 'objects' with compositions in which figures and natural forms are only mildly distorted was one of Gauguin's most effective and consistent narrative strategies.

Fig.60 <u>Pont-Aven, Village Drama</u> 1894
Oil on canvas
73 x 92
Private Collection,
whereabouts unknown

113

43
The Breton Shepherdess 1886
Oil on canvas
61 x 74
Laing Art Gallery, Newcastle
upon Tyne (Tyne & Wear
Archives and Museums)

44
*Breton Woman from Pont-Aven
in Profile* 1886
Watercolour on paper laid down
on cardboard
20 x 14
Galerie Charles Bailly, Paris

45
Comings and Goings, Martinique 1887
Oil on canvas
72.5 x 92
Carmen Thyssen-Bornemisza Collection,
on loan at the Thyssen-Bornemisza
Museum, Madrid

46
Study of Martiniquaises 1887
Pastel and charcoal on paper
41.9 x 53.6
Private Collection, Moscow

48
Breton Girls Dancing, Pont-Aven 1888
Oil on canvas
73 x 92.7
National Gallery of Art, Washington.
Collection of Mr and Mrs Paul Mellon

47
Breton Girls Dancing, Pont-Aven 1888
Pastel, charcoal, watercolour and gouache
on paper
58.6 x 41.9
The Morgan Library & Museum,
New York. Thaw Collection

49
Carved Cane *1888–90*
Boxwood, mother-of-pearl and iron
h.93.3
The Metropolitan Museum of Art, New
York. Bequest of Adelaide Milton de Groot
(1876–1967), 1967

50
Gauguin's Wooden Shoes *1889–90*
Polychromed oak, leather, and iron nails
Each 12.9 x 32.7 x 11.3
National Gallery of Art, Washington.
Chester Dale Collection, 1963

51
Cow on the Cliffs of Porsac'h or
Over the Abyss *1888*
Oil on canvas
73 x 60
Musée des Arts Décoratifs, Paris

119

58
Black Pigs 1891
Oil on canvas
91 x 72
Szépmuvészeti Múzeum, Budapest

59
Tahitians c.1891
Oil, crayon and charcoal on paper
mounted on millboard
85.4 x 101.9
Tate. Presented by the Contemporary
Art Society 1917

'You must think I speak too much about pigs: what's to be done you see them in every corner and they are part of the character of the country. I need to explain that in former times they were cannibals and the missionaries introduced the pig whose flesh tastes like that of a human being in order to break them of this bad habit. In a corner of the painting this inscription – E. haere maï ta maha – Come Eat'
Letter from Gauguin to his wife, spring 1892

60
Haere Mai 1891
Oil on burlap
72.4 x 91.4
Solomon R. Guggenheim Museum,
New York, Thannhauser Collection.
Gift of Justin K. Thannhauser, 1978

61
Tahitian Landscape 1891
Oil on canvas
67.9 x 92.4
The Minneapolis Institute of Arts.
The Julius C. Eliel Memorial Fund

65
Vision of the Sermon (Jacob Wrestling with the Angel) 1888
Oil on canvas
73 x 92
National Gallery of Scotland, Edinburgh

66
Nativity (Bébé) c.1896
Oil on canvas
67 x 76.5
*The State Hermitage Museum,
St Petersburg*

67
Breton Calvary (The Green Christ)
1889
Oil on canvas
92 x 73.5
Royal Museums of Fine Arts of
Belgium, Brussels

68
The Yellow Christ 1889
Oil on canvas
92.1 x 73.3
Albright-Knox Art Gallery Buffalo, NY.
General Purchase Funds, 1946

69
Sketch for 'The Yellow Christ' 1889
Pencil on paper
26.7 x 18.2
Carmen Thyssen-Bornemisza Collection,
on loan at the Thyssen-Bornemisza
Museum, Madrid

84
Maternity / Women by the Sea 1899
Oil on canvas
95.5 x 73.5
The State Hermitage Museum,
St Petersburg

85
The Bark (La Barque) 1896
Oil on canvas
50.5 x 37.5
Courtesy of Mr Giammarco Cappuzzo

86
*Te Pape Nave Nave
(Delectable Waters)* 1898
*Oil on canvas
74 x 95.3
National Gallery of Art,
Washington. Collection of
Mr and Mrs Paul Mellon*

87
Parahi te Marae (Là réside le Temple /
There Lies the Temple) 1892
Oil on canvas
66 x 88.9
Philadelphia Museum of Art. Gift
of Mr and Mrs Rodolphe Meyer de
Schauensee, 1980

this particular sheet suggests the concept for the journal may have been much earlier. Under the heading 'L'Immorale', Gauguin penned a tongue-in-cheek review of a shocking, and surely imaginary, play performed by the 'Grand Théâtre National de Bora Bora'. The central character was Anna Demonio, whose practice of free love without emotional attachment ended with an act of incest resulting in a monstrous androgynous conception: 'And the monster strangling its creature fecundates spacious loins with its seed, thereby engendering Seraphitus Seraphita.' This gnomic phrase, which Gauguin repeated at the end of the review, was a reference to Honoré de Balzac's *Seraphita*, the curious mystical novel about androgyny in which, according to Morice, Gauguin contrived to find 'the whole of Balzac'. Although the text may explain the ambiguous gender of Gauguin's *Oviri*, there is nothing in Balzac to explain the sculpture's animalistic violence. This may allude, rather, to the former practice of infanticide among the Areoi, Tahiti's priestly elite, a practice that missionary workers in the region had by and large eradicated.[16]

Prior to modelling his stoneware sculpture, Gauguin first introduced his Oviri motif into a Tahitian genre painting from 1892, *E haere oe i hia* (*Where Are You Going?*) (no.115), producing a powerful, defamiliarising effect that is more disturbing than the near-identical composition *Eu haere ia oe* (*Where Are You Going?* or *Woman Holding a Fruit*) (no.122). Back in Paris, Gauguin made use of Ernest Chaplet's studio and kiln to model the statue. As June Hargrove and others have observed, the final realisation, at the formal and conceptual level, invites comparison with Auguste Rodin's statue of *Balzac*, a major project that was giving Rodin considerable trouble just at that date.[17] *Oviri*'s fluid forms, particularly when seen from the back, where the flow of hair divides into labial folds, are strangely similar to the voluminous cloak swathing the body of Balzac in Rodin's statue, and both works have a phallic dimension. Whether or not Gauguin could have had a clear idea of what Rodin's *Balzac* looked like, since it was not completed until 1898, Rodin's concurrent commission was on his mind: discussing with Morice how he would have set about sculpting Balzac, Gauguin stated that he would have shown the author holding in his palm his androgynous creatures, Seraphitus and Seraphita.

Gauguin's exhibition of his sculpture and ceramics at the 'Les XX' exhibition in Brussels in 1891 (including his *Eve* and two major wood carvings *Soyez amoureuses* and *Soyez mystérieuses*) provoked a critical storm in the city. When he submitted *Oviri* to the committee of the Salon de la Société Nationale des Beaux-Arts in Paris in 1895, it was refused admission, perhaps to pre-empt a repetition of the earlier furore. This rejection was surprising given the Salon's generally liberal attitudes toward decorative art objects: overtly erotic hybrid work like the sculpted furniture of Rupert Carabin was shown, for instance. The reason surely lay in *Oviri*'s incomprehensible ugliness. For Gauguin it was a crushing blow.

The Oviri idea would not rest. Gauguin revisited it in two watercolour monotypes (nos.109, 111) and he also reworked it in a woodcut, which he inserted into the text of *Noa Noa* (no.110). Although he left the stoneware sculpture behind in France, later he wrote to de Monfreid asking for it to be sent out to Polynesia so it could be placed on his tomb. This wish was ultimately realised, but with a bronze cast as the stoneware would not have survived the humid Marquesan climate. *Oviri* was manifestly some sort of alter ego, a female self – at once creative, mysterious and dreaming as well as destructive, monstrously cruel. Certainly Morice saw it that way and he was probably party to the artist's wishes: he described *Oviri* as a kind of Diana or Hina the huntress.[18] In the evolution of this hauntingly uncanny image we have an illuminating example of Gauguin's creative intelligence at work. *Oviri* was a project of many facets in which the artist engaged in a personal confrontation with his heroes and rivals in literature, painting and sculpture – Balzac, Delacroix and Rodin.

89
Study for 'In the Heat (Pigs) / En Pleine Chaleur (Cochons)' 1888
Pastel, watercolour and ink on paper
26.3 x 40.4
Van Gogh Museum, Amsterdam
(Vincent van Gogh Foundation)

90
The Bathing Place 1889
Gouache, watercolour, pastel and gold
paint on paper mounted on panel
34.5 x 45
Private Collection

91
Life and Death 1889
Oil on canvas
93 x 75
Musée Mahmoud Khalil, Giza

160

92
Ondine / In the Waves 1889
Oil on fabric
92.5 x 72.4
The Cleveland Museum of Art. Gift of
Mr and Mrs William Powell Jones

108
Pape Moe *1894*
Wood carving bas-relief on oak
73 x 55 x 5
Sandro and Marta Bosi Collection

171

109
Oviri 1894
Watercolour trace monotype on paper
29.3 x 20.7
Harvard Art Museum / Fogg Museum,
Cambridge, MA. Gift of the Woodner
Family Collection, Inc.

111
Oviri 1894
Watercolour monotype on paper
28.2 x 22.2
Private Collection

110
Oviri 1894–5
Colour woodcut
20.4 x 12.2
National Gallery of Art, Washington.
Rosenwald Collection, 1953

Oviri 1894
Stoneware
75 x 19 x 27
Musée d'Orsay, Paris

'I have just finished a severed kanak head nicely arranged on a white cushion in a palace of my invention and guarded by women also of my invention. I believe that it is a pretty piece of painting. It is not entirely mine since I stole it from a plank of pine. Don't tell anyone but what do you want, one does what one can, and when marble or wood draws a head for you it's very tempting to steal.'
Letter to Daniel de Monfreid, June 1892

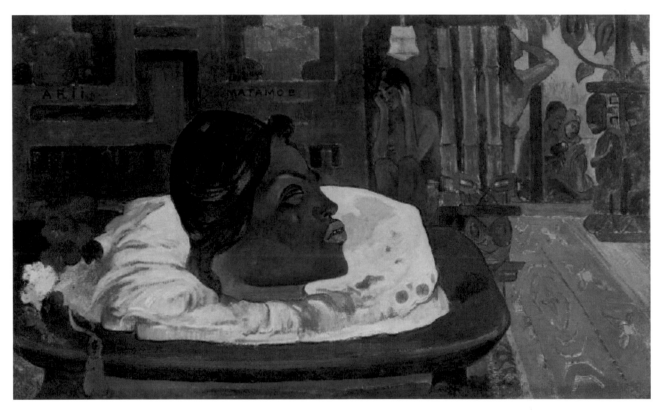

117
Arii Matamoe (La Fin royale / The Royal End) 1892
Oil on coarse fabric
45 x 75
J. Paul Getty Museum, Los Angeles

182

'With a simple nude I intended to suggest a certain savage luxuriousness of a bygone age. The whole painting is bathed in deliberately sombre, sad colours; it is neither silk nor velvet, neither batiste nor gold that creates this luxury, but rather the paint surface enriched by the artist's hand. No fancifulness ... solely the imagination of a man has enriched this interior with his fantasy. The title is Nevermore; it is not Edgar Poe's raven keeping watch, but the Devil's bird ...'
Letter to Daniel de Monfreid, 14 February 1897

'Do you remember reproaching me for having put a title on that painting: don't you think that that title Nevermore lay behind this acquisition – Perhaps! Be that as it may, I am delighted that Delius should be its owner, given that it wasn't a speculative purchase for resale, but because he fell in love with it; then another time he will want to buy a second, especially if people who come to visit him compliment him on it, or all the more so enter into a discussion with him about it.'
Letter to Daniel de Monfreid, 12 January 1899

118
<u>Nevermore O Tahiti</u> *1897*
Oil on canvas
60.5 x 116
The Samuel Courtauld Trust, The
Courtauld Gallery, London

124
The Artist's Portfolio 1894
*Two inside covers decorated in watercolour,
gouache, charcoal and pencil on paper sewn
to leather, leather binding inscribed in pen
and ink with additions in watercolour; silk
ribbons stitched into binding*
42.5 x 26.4
*The Metropolitan Museum of Art, New
York. Promised Gift of Leon D. and Debra
R. Black, and Purchase, Joseph Pulitzer
and Florence B. Seldon Bequests, and 1999
Benefit Fund, 2000*

TELLER OF TALES

In Gauguin's book *Noa Noa* the arcane refrain 'Le Conteur parle' punctuates the text, introducing the sections penned by the artist – the 'I' of the narrative – as distinct from the insertions written in the third person by the 'poet', Charles Morice. The book closes with the words: 'Le Conteur achève son récit' ('The Teller of Tales concludes his narrative', see fig.41).[1] This arch stance as Teller of Tales is not without suggestive implications for the way Gauguin approached his art as a whole and, in particular, his work in the various graphic media.

For Gauguin *Noa Noa* realised a long-standing fascination with works that combine text and image. His appreciation in the mid-1880s of the contemporary artist-illustrators Randolph Caldecott and Boutet de Monvel informed his ceramic designs and also fed into the Volpini suite, his first serious undertaking as a maker of prints (no.125). Produced on the advice of his dealer Theo van Gogh, the album, comprising ten zincographs and a cover sheet, reprised subjects from his recent paintings; it was put on show with them at Monsieur Volpini's café at the 1889 Exposition Universelle in Paris. The prints are often captioned, and venture into new narrative territory.[2] A previously unsuspected excursion into the comic-strip genre recently came to light – a collaborative venture undertaken that same year in Brittany in which, together with Charles Laval and others, Gauguin compiled, for a child's amusement, an album of 'Istoyres' (fig.71).[3]

Gauguin had already produced a template, or sourcebook, for *Noa Noa* in the form of *Ancien Culte mahorie* (fig.72), whose text was wholly, if selectively, copied from J.-A. Moerenhout, sometimes verbatim, sometimes in summary form.[4] The transcribed legends informed a number of the paintings from the first Tahitian voyage, while the list of Tahitian words doubtless helped Gauguin devise his Tahitian titles. *Ancien Culte mahorie* also has beautiful embellishments in the form of vivid ink and watercolour illustrations, which occasionally borrow Marquesan decorative patterns (fig.31); they made their way, scarcely altered, into Gauguin's personal version of the *Noa Noa* text (now in the Louvre), on which he worked in Tahiti (no.128).

Gauguin's period of enforced immobility in Pont-Aven in 1894, following an ankle injury, was highly productive. This was possibly the moment when he started the scrapbook that became *Cahier pour Aline* (no.126). It remained a private production which, sadly, his daughter never received. Embellished with a haunting cover, it is partly a book of press cuttings relating to his

Fig.71 *From an album of drawings produced for the young Jacques Bousquet, Pont-Aven or Le Pouldu 1889–90* <u>Cuite d'Istoyres illustré par Gauguin et de Laval et M. Jacques et Jourdan</u>
Pencil on paper
Private Collection

1893 exhibition, partly a series of philosophical and political reflections. Gauguin also embarked on a series of watercolour monotypes, some of his most inventive and delicate works in the graphic medium, mining and freely combining the rich seam of imagery offered by memories of his recent Tahitian paintings

132
Te Arii Vahine – Opoi (Lady of Royal
Blood – Fatigue) 1898
Woodcut on paper
17.1 x 30.4
National Gallery of Art, Washington.
Rosenwald Collection, 1948

133
Soyez amoureuses, vous serez heureuses (Be
in Love and You Will be Happy) 1898
Woodcut on paper
16.2 x 27.6
National Gallery of Art, Washington.
Rosenwald Collection, 1950

134
Le Sourire 1900
Title sheet
Woodcut inscribed in pen and ink
32 x 23.6
The Art Institute of Chicago.
Print sales Miscellaneous Fund

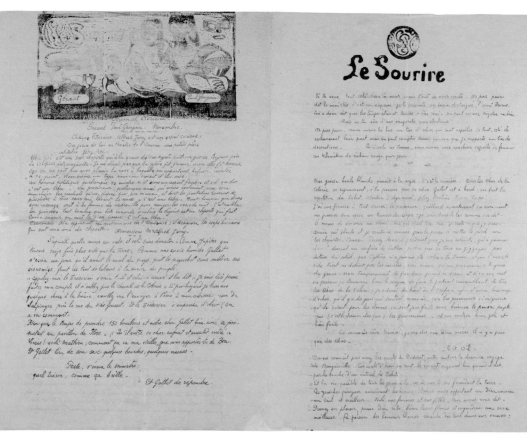

135
Le Sourire, Journal Sérieux
November 1899
Woodcut, monogram, hand-
written text and mimeograph
illustrations on paper
39.7 x 25.5
The Art Institute of Chicago.
Mr and Mrs Carter H.
Harrison Collection

Le Sourire

Writing and journalism ran in Gauguin's family, penned by his maternal grandmother Flora Tristan and his father Clovis. When jaded with what Tahiti had to offer as pictorial inspiration, Gauguin turned his attention to politics and satire. He wrote tracts attacking the institutions of the Catholic Church and marriage. As well as penning waspish journalism for *Les Guêpes*, an organ of the Catholic Party and owned by local politician François Cardella, Gauguin also worked solo on *Le Sourire*. Cyclostyled using a method devised by Thomas Edison, the journal – with a print run of about thirty copies – was probably modelled on such

polemical and satirical journals as Jean-Louis Forain's short-lived *Le Fifre*, which Gauguin enjoyed during the 1889 Exposition Universelle. *Le Sourire* – a sort of colonial *Private Eye* – is chiefly valued today for its inventive woodcut mastheads and illustrations; its highly localised articles deal with venality among local traders and administrators, Gauguin hiding his serious intent behind a jokey tone. The November 1899 issue (no.135) features appreciative references to other satirical works, Alfred Jarry's *Ubu Roi* (1896) and Diderot's *Supplément au Voyage de Bougainville* (1772).

136
Le Sourire, Journal Sérieux
19 September 1899
Woodcut, monogram, hand-written text and mimeograph illustrations on paper
34.9 x 26
The Art Institute of Chicago. Mr and Mrs Carter H. Harrison Collection

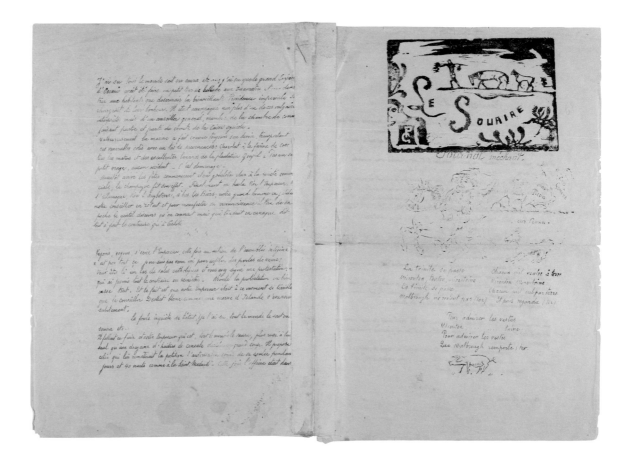

144
Tahitian Faces c.1899
Charcoal on paper
41 x 31.1
The Metropolitan Museum of Art,
New York. Purchase, The Annenberg
Foundation Gift, 1996

145
Two Tahitian Women 1899
Oil on canvas
94 x 72.4
The Metropolitan Museum of Art,
New York. Gift of William Church
Osborn, 1949

215

155

Maison du jouir (House of Pleasure)
1901–2 Five carved door panels from
Gauguin's Atuona residence (Marquesas)
Polychromed sequoia wood
Musée d'Orsay, Paris

Left to right: Soyez mystérieuses 32 x 153
x 3; Nude woman and small dog 200 x
39.8 x 2.5; Maison du Jouir 40 x 24.4 x 2.3;
Nude woman and tree with red fruits 159
x 40 x 2.5; Soyez amoureuses et vous serez
heureuses 45 x 204.5 x 2.2

Paris 1889, p.25. The quotation follows from a *Conférence sur Tahiti* by M. Théophile Van der Veene. The long quote was in fact taken from E. Raoul's book, *Tahiti*. Gauguin muddled the footnotes.

25. He only thinks of going to French territories or colonies: Martinique, Madagascar, Tahiti.

26. 'Puisse venir le jour (et peut-être bientôt), où j'irai m'enfuir dans les bois sur une île de l'Océanie, vivre là d'extase, de calme et d'art. Entouré d'une nouvelle famille, loin de cette lutte européenne après l'argent.' Paul Gauguin, letter to Mette, February 1890, ed. Malingue 1946, letter C, p.184.

27. Delacroix went to Morocco in 1832 as part of a diplomatic mission; Prosper Marilhat accompanied a scientific mission; Louis Garneray, Alexandre Decamps and Horace Vernet followed military expeditions. According to the official order from the French government, Gauguin's mission consisted in 'studying from the point of view of art and painting in order to understand the customs and landscape of this country'.

28. 'Quand je reviendrai, j'aurai de quoi fournir à la clientèle . . . Je sens que je commence à posséder le caractère océanien et je puis assurer que ce que je fais ici n'a été fait par personne et qu'on ne connaît pas en France cela.' Paul Gauguin, letter to Mette, June 1892, in Malingue 1946, no. CXXIX, p.227.

29. 'Je t'écris ce soir. Ce silence de la nuit à Tahiti est encore plus étrange que le reste. Il n'existe que là, sans un cri d'oiseau pour troubler le repos . . . Les indigènes circulent souvent la nuit, mais pieds nus et silencieux. Toujours ce silence. Je comprends pourquoi ces individus peuvent rester des heures, des journées assis sans dire un mot et regarder le ciel avec mélancolie. Je sens que tout cela va m'envahir.' Paul Gauguin, letter to Mette, July 1891, in Malingue 1946, no. CXXVI, p.218.

30. 'Au bord de la mer, une belle case en bois, enveloppée de tous ces arbres bizarres et luisants dont j'ai oublié les noms . . . dans l'atmosphère une odeur enivrante, indéfinissable . . . autour de nous, au-delà de la chambre éclairée d'une lumière rose tamisée par des stores, décorée de nattes fraîches et de fleurs capiteuses.' Charles Baudelaire, '*Les Projets*', in *Le Spleen de Paris: oeuvres complètes*, Claude Pichois, ed., Bibliothèque de la Pleiade, vol.I, Paris 1975, pp.314–15. This quotation from Baudelaire's poem, an extract from a press cutting, was stuck by Gauguin into *Diverses choses*, see fig.20.

31. See *Zoos humains*, Nicolas Blancel, Pascal Blanchard, Gilles Boëtsch, Eric Deroo, Sandrine Lemaire, eds., Paris 2004.

32. 'Le sol Tahitien devient tout à fait français, et petit à petit tout cet ancien état des choses va disparaître.' Paul Gauguin, letter to Mette, July 1891, in Malingue 1946, no.CXXVI, p.219.

33. 'En somme, l'Orient n'approche pas de ce rêve éveillé que j'en avais fait il y a deux ans, ou bien c'est que cet Orient-là est encore plus loin ou plus haut, j'en ai assez de courir après la poésie; je crois qu'elle est à votre porte, et peut-être dans votre lit. Moi je suis encore l'homme qui court, mais je vais tâcher de m'arrêter et d'attendre.' Gérard de Nerval, letter to Jules Janin, written on his return from his journey to the Orient, 'on the boat, near Malta', ('en mer, près de Malte') 16 November 1843, in *Oeuvres complètes: voyage en Orient*, vol.II, Paris 1989, p.1,407.

34. 'Mon centre artistique est dans mon cerveau.' Paul Gauguin, letter to Mette, March 1892, ed. Malingue 1946, letter CXXVII, p.221.

35. 'L'expérience que j'ai faite à la Martinique est décisive. Là seulement je me suis senti vraiment *moi-même*, et c'est dans ce que j'en ai rapporté qu'il faut me chercher, si l'on veut savoir qui je suis, plus encore que dans mes œuvres de Bretagne.' Reported by Charles Morice, in *Gauguin*, Paris 1920, p.88.

36. 'ce que je désire, c'est un coin de moi-même encore inconnu', Paul Gauguin, letter to Émile Bernard, August 1889, ed. Malingue 1946, letter LXXXIV, p.163.

37. 'une des plus importantes richesses spirituelles que j'étais venu chercher à Tahiti', Paul Gauguin, *Noa Noa,* manuscript in the Louvre, Paris, fol.79 verso.

38. 'C'est que l'homme ne peut changer le fond de son cœur. Les objets extérieurs peuvent le distraire un moment, mais ce qui l'occupera sans cesse, ce qui se présentera sans cesse à lui, c'est son intérieur, ce sont les rêveries accoutumées de son âme. Après avoir été errant quelques moments hors de lui-même, il rentre pour ainsi dire dans son cœur.' François-René de Chateaubriand, 'Journal de Jérusalem', quoted by André Guyaux, 'Le Voyageur désabusé', in *Orients littéraires*, Paris 2004, pp.165–85.

39. 'J'apprends que M. Paul Gauguin va partir pour Tahiti. Son intention est de vivre là plusieurs années, seul, d'y construire sa hutte, d'y travailler à neuf des choses qui le hantent. Le cas d'un homme fuyant la civilisation, recherchant volontairement l'oubli et le silence pour mieux se sentir, pour mieux écouter les voix intérieures qui s'étouffent au bruit de nos passions et de nos disputes m'a paru curieux et troublant . . .'. Octave Mirbeau, 'Paul Gauguin', *Echo de Paris*, 16 February 1891.

40. 'la difficulté de gagner *régulièrement* ma vie malgré ma réputation, mon goût pour l'exotique aidant, m'ont fait prendre une détermination irrévocable . . . Je repars pour l'Océanie . . . Rien ne m'empêchera de partir et ce sera pour toujours. Quelle bête existence que l'européenne vie [sic].' Paul Gauguin, letter to William Molard, September 1894, ed. Malingue 1946, no.CLII, p.260.

41. 'depuis mon projet de m'enterrer aux îles du Pacifique', Paul Gauguin, letter to Maurice Denis, March 1895, ed. Malingue 1946, no.CLVII, p.267.

42. 'Je suis en train d'organiser ma vie pour me désintéresser de plus en plus de la peinture, me retirer, comme on dit, de la scène en faisant des travaux d'écriture à Tahiti soit avec un peu d'agriculture sur mon terrain.' Paul Gauguin, letter mistakenly described as being to Emmanuel Bibesco, May 1900, ed. Malingue 1946, no.CLXXIII, p.295. In fact the recipient was the dealer A. Vollard and the date Jan. 1900. See Rewald 1986, pp.189–92.

43. 'Je suis à terre aujourd'hui, vaincu par la misère et surtout la maladie d'une vieillesse tout à fait prématurée. Aurai-je quelque répit pour terminer mon œuvre, je n'ose l'espérer: en tout cas je fais un dernier effort en allant le mois prochain m'installer à Fatu-iva, île des Marquises presqu'encore anthropophage. Je crois que là, cet élément tout à fait sauvage, cette solitude complète me donnera avant de mourir un dernier feu d'enthousiasme qui rajeunira mon imagination et fera la conclusion de mon talent.' Paul Gauguin, letter to Charles Morice, July 1901, ed. Malingue 1946, no.CLXXIV, p.300.

44. Note the difference that exists between, for example, certain photos of Tahitian men and women by Charles Spitz (e.g. fig.38), Henri Lemasson or Hoare, which the ethnologists classify under the title 'Types and costumes', and the works they inspired Gauguin to paint.

45. 'L'étoile route et le Désir de l'Orient – l'Europe . . . – le rêve se réalise – Les mers – souvenirs débrouillés à travers . . . Les hommes m'ont fait souffrir – Climat où ma tête repose – Amours laissés dans un tombeau – Elle, je l'avais perdue – . . . – Vaisseau d'Orient'. Gérard de Nerval, *Carnet du Caire*, in *Oeuvres complètes*, eds. Pichois and Guillaume, vol.II, Paris 1984, p.853.

46. 'L'idole est là non comme une explication littéraire, mais comme une statue, moins statue peut-être que les figures animales; moins animale aussi, faisant corps dans mon rêve, devant ma case, avec la nature entière, régnant *en notre âme primitive*, consolation imaginaire de nos souffrances en ce qu'elles comportent de vague et d'incompris devant le mystère de notre origine et de notre avenir.' Paul Gauguin, letter to André Fontainas, March 1899, ed. Malingue 1946, no.CLXX, p.288–9.

47. The critic of *L'Escarmouche* reproached him in 1893 for not being a real Tahitian painter: 'This travesty of a civilised man who masters his paintbrush so well makes us smile . . . we await the arrival in Paris of a real Tahitian painter who lives at the jardin d'acclimatation whilst his paintings are shown at Durand-Ruel's. A real Maori in fact!' ('Ce travesti d'un civilisé très maître de son pinceau nous fait sourire . . . nous attendons l'arrivée à Paris d'un vrai peintre tahitien qui, tandis que son œuvre sera chez Durand-Ruel ou ailleurs, logera au jardin d'acclimatation. Un vrai maorie. Quoi!'). *L'Escarmouche*, 19 November 1893. The article is pasted into Paul Gauguin's *Cahier pour Aline*.

48. 'Vous êtes actuellement cet artiste inouï, légendaire, qui du fond de l'Océanie envoie des oeuvres déconcertantes, inimitables, oeuvres définitives d'un grand homme pour ainsi dire disparu du monde . . . Bref, vous jouissez de l'immunité des grands morts, vous êtes passé dans l'Histoire de l'art.' Letter from George-Daniel de Monfreid to Paul Gauguin, 11 December 1902, in Joly-Segalen 1950, p.233.

49. 'Pas plus tard que cette nuit j'ai rêvé que j'étais mort et chose curieuse, c'était le moment vrai où je vivais heureux.' Paul Gauguin, *Avant et après*, reprinted in Guérin 1974, p.341.

Gauguin and Segalen: Exoticism, Myth and the 'Aesthetics of Diversity'
Charles Forsdick pp.56–63

1. For an introduction to Segalen, see Charles Forsdick, *Victor Segalen and the Aesthetics of Diversity: Journeys between Cultures*, Oxford 2000, and also Marie Dollé, *Victor Segalen: le voyageur incertain*, Croissy-Beaubourg 2008, and Gilles Manceron, *Segalen*, Paris 1992.

2. See James Clifford, 'A Poetics of Displacement: Victor Segalen', in *The Predicament of Culture: Twentieth-Century Ethnography, Literature and Art*, Cambridge, MA 1988, pp.152–63 (p.152).

3. Clifford 1988, p.152.

4. Victor Segalen, *Oeuvres complètes*, ed. Henry Bouillier, 2 vols, Paris 1995. These were published by Laffont and follow this pattern of cycles to structure Gauguin's works.

5. Gauguin inspired Segalen's first published literary work, the 1904 *Mercure de France* article entitled 'Gauguin dans son dernier décor', and he continued writing about the artist until his death in 1919. At the request of George-Daniel de Monfreid, he drafted an introduction to a new edition of *Noa Noa*, but this did not appear as a result of the First World War; Gauguin was also the subject of one of his final works, 'Hommage à Gauguin', published as the preface to a collection of letters from the artist to de Monfreid in 1918. (Segalen completed correction of the proofs of this work in January of that year, while he was still in China, recruiting Chinese workers to serve on the Western Front.)

6. David Sweetman, *Paul Gauguin: A Complete Life*, London 1995, p.539.

7. Victor Segalen, *Correspondance I, 1893–1912*, ed. Henry Bouillier, Paris 2004, p.527. Unless otherwise stated, all translations are my own.

8. On Gouzer, see Manceron 1992, pp.159–60, and Sweetman 1995, pp.443–4.

9. Victor Segalen, 'Hommage à Gauguin', *Oeuvres complètes*, Paris 1995, vol.I, pp.349–73.

10. Sweetman 1995, p.539.

11. For a discussion of these texts and their respective fates, see Manceron 1992, pp.162–4.

12. The original *Cahier* is now in the Bibliothèque de l'INHA (collections Jacques Doucet; mss.227). A facsimile was published in two volumes by the Société des amis de la Bibliothèque d'art et d'archéologie de l'Université de Paris in 1963. A copy is available online at: http://www.inha.fr/.

13. Victor Segalen, *Les Immémoriaux*, Paris 1907. For an English version, see *Lapse of Memory*, trans. Rosemary Arnoux, Brisbane 1995. Gilles Manceron recounts how Segalen heard the genealogical narrative with which the novel begins at Paul Vernier's house on Hiva-Oa. See Manceron 1992, pp.170–1.

14. Segalen's basic monthly salary was 243 francs and 90 centimes, of which his purchases at the auction amounted to 188 francs and 95 centimes.

15. Manceron 1992, p.185.

16. Segalen, 'Hommage à Gauguin', p.371. See also G. Wildenstein, 'Inventaire des biens' and 'Vente' in *Gauguin, sa vie, son oeuvre: documents inédits*, Paris 1958, pp.201–9.

17. These expressions are used in a letter (August 1903) to Louise Ponty, a friend of Segalen's from Bordeaux and cousin of philosopher Maurice Merleau-Ponty, Victor Segalen, *Correspondance I, 1893–1912*, pp.534–5.

18. Segalen purchased only four of these, with the fifth being acquired by an unknown bidder; it was only in 1990 that the set was reunited when the Musée d'Orsay acquired the fifth panel and was able to add it to those purchased by the French state from the Segalen family in 1952. For a detailed account of the auction, see Manceron 1992, pp.183–91. Details of the lots dispersed are included in H. Jacquier, 'Le Dossier de la succession Paul Gauguin', *Bulletin de la société des études océaniennes*, vol.120, 1959, pp.673–711.

19. Segalen, 'Hommage à Gauguin', p.373.

20. Victor Segalen, *Journal des îles*, in Bouillier 1995, pp.396–479 (p.429).

21. Sweetman 1995, p.539.

22. Arsène Alexandre was the first to suggest in 1930 that the picture had in fact not been painted in the Pacific but in Brittany, and subsequent scientific analyses of Gauguin's palette have proved that Segalen's hypothesis of a nostalgic artist longing for a snow-covered landscape was flawed; meteorological studies suggest that it seems most likely that the canvas was painted in 1889 or 1890. See Mauricette Berne, ed., *Victor Segalen: voyageur et visionnaire*, Paris 1999, p.50.

23. Victor Segalen, 'Gauguin dans son dernier décor', in *Oeuvres complètes*, ed. Bouillier 1995, vol.I (p.291).

24. Letter from Segalen to Jules de Gaultier, 18 October 1907, *Correspondance I, 1893–1912*, ed. Bouillier 2004, p.717.

25. Stephen F. Eisenman, *Gauguin's Skirt*, New York 1997, p.195.

26. Segalen 1995, vol.I, pp.361–2.

27. Letter from Segalen to George-Daniel de Monfreid, 12 April 1906, *Correspondance I, 1893–1912*, ed. Bouillier 2004, p.660.

Gauguin: A Very British Reception
Amy Dickson pp.64–9

1. Bullen Introduction, in J.B. Bullen, ed., *Post-Impressionists in England: The Critical Reception*, London 1988, p.1.

2. Fry's letter to his father, 24 November 1910, reproduced in Sutton Denys, *Letters of Roger Fry*, 1972, quoted in Anna Gruetzner Robins, *Modern Art in Britain 1910–1914*, London 1997, p.15.

3. Robert Ross, 'The Post-Impressionists at the Grafton: The Twilight of the Idols', *Morning Post*, 7 November 1910, three reviews reproduced in Bullen 1988, p.100.

4. Gruetzner Robins 1997.

5. Spencer Frederick Gore, 'Cezanne, Gauguin, Van Gogh &c., at the Grafton Galleries', in Bullen 1988, p.141.

6. *Manao tupapau* was listed in the 'Manet and the Post-Impressionists' catalogue as *L'Esprit Veille*.

7. 'Manet and the Post-Impressionists' catalogue, London 1910, and Gruetzner Robins 1997, p.28.

8. Unsigned review 'Paint Run Mad' in *Daily Express*, 9 November 1910 in Bullen 1988, pp.105–6.

9. J.B. Bullen, 'Great British Gauguin: His Reception in London in 1910–11', in *Apollo*, October 2003, p.4.

10. Gruetzner Robins 1997, p.29.

11. Gruetzner Robins makes this observation in Gruetzner Robins 1997, p.29.

12. C. Lewis Hind, *The Post-Impressionists*, London 1911, quoted in Gruetzner Robins 1997, p.29.

13. Laurence Binyon, 'Post Impressionists', *Saturday Review*, 12 November 1910, pp.609–10, in Bullen 1988, p.112.

14. Julius Meier-Graefe, *Modern Art: Being a Contribution to a New System of Aesthetics*, 1904 (trans. London 1908), p.63.

15. Joly-Segalen 1950, XLII, April 1898, pp.122–3, cited in Gloria Groom, 'Chronology: July 1895–November 1903', in *The Art of Paul Gauguin*, exh. cat., Chicago 1988, p.382.

16. Joly-Segalen 1950, pp.122–3.

17. M. Fayet se trouve en relations avec un écrivain qui va faire une étude sur vous (et sur d'autres artistes, je crois, tels que Degas, Renoir, etc. . .) Meier-Graef [sic], si je ne me trompe. Il va peut-être publier dans son livre votre manuscrit primitivement destiné au "Mercure de France". Je verrai cela de près et vous tiendrai au courant, de toute façon. Joly-Segalen 1950, p.241. The text to which he refers was probably *Racontars de rapin*, which Gauguin sent to Fontainas in September 1902.

18. Britt Salvesen, *Artists In Focus: Gauguin*, The Art Institute of Chicago, 2001, p.8.

19. Unsigned Review, 'An Art Victory: Triumphant Exit of the Post-Impressionists', *Daily Graphic*, 16 January 1911, p.15, in Bullen 1988, p.184.

20. J.B. M[anson], 'The Paintings of Cézanne and Gauguin' in *Outlook*, 2 December 1911, pp.785–6 in Bullen 1988, p.245.

21. Nicola Morby identified the figures in *Gauguin and Connoisseurs* in her catalogue entry no.2 in Robert Upstone (ed.), *Modern Painters: The Camden Town Group*, exh. cat. Tate, London 2008.

22. Sadler's notes from a conversation on 27 September 1911 with John Nevill, the new director of the Stafford Gallery, suggest that the 1911 exhibition was his son Michael's idea: 'I urged him [Nevill] (following up Michael's previous suggestion to him) to have next November a small carefully selected exhibition of fine pictures by Gauguin and Cézanne at his Gallery.' Conversation with Mr John Nevill, Stafford Gallery – Michael Sadler Archive/TGA 8221.5.23, as referred to by Frances Fowle in her essay, 'Following the Vision: From Brittany to Edinburgh', in Thomson 2005, p.108.

23. My thanks to Belinda Thomson for drawing my attention to these.

24. Bullen has argued that too much emphasis has been placed on the 1910 exhibition.

25. Susan Stein, 'From the Beginning: Collecting and Exhibiting Gauguin in New York', in *Lure of the Exotic: Gauguin in New York Collections*, Yale 2002.

26. *Exposition Paul Gauguin Galerie Ambroise Vollard*, exhibition catalogue, Paris 1903; also in Gloria Groom's chronology in the Chicago catalogue, p.387.

27. *The Times*, 9 October 1906, paraphrased in Bullen 1988, pp.6–7.

28. *The International Society of Sculptors, Painters and Gravers Art Congress. The Catalogue of The Eighth Exhibition*, London 1908. *Haere-Pape, Tahiti* is listed as hanging in the 'balcony' and is item 410 in the catalogue. Roger Fry's response to the Burlington editorial, published in the March 1908 issue of the same publication, refers to two further Gauguins, 'Femmes Maories' and 'Te Arti Vahine' [sic]. As these were not included in the 1908 show or illustrated in Meier-Graefe's *Modern Art*, it seems most likely that Fry had seen these in the 1906 Paris exhibition.

29. Unsigned review (probably by Roger Fry), 'Modern French Pictures at Brighton', in *The Times*, 11 July 1910, p.12, in Bullen 1988, pp.89–90.

30. Henry McBride, 'Gauguin's Rebirth', *The Dial*, vol.69, July–December 1920, pp.397–400, quoted in Stein 2002, p.161.

31. Maugham and O'Conor frequented the Chat Blanc in Montparnasse at this date, together with a large Anglophone group of artists – Gauguin was one of the artists they most admired.

32. W. Somerset Maugham, *Of Human Bondage*, in the Modern Library Paperback edition, 1999, chapter 44, p.370.

33. Frances Fowle, 'Following the Vision: From Brittany to Edinburgh', in Thomson 2005, p.108.

34. Edward Marsh, *The Collected Poems of Rupert Brooke: With a Memoir*, 1918, p.civ. Belinda Thomson drew my attention to this.

35. Richard Albert Cordell, *Somerset Maugham, A Writer for all Seasons*, London 1962.

36. Meier-Graefe 1908, p.63.

37. W. Somerset Maugham, *The Moon and Sixpence*, London 1919, reprinted 1999, p.1.

38. Letter to Mette, Tahiti, c. March 1892, in Malingue 1946, CXXVII, p.223.

39. J. David Macey Jr. makes the case for multiple narrators in his essay 'Fantasy as Necessity: The Role of the Biographer in *The Moon and Sixpence*', *Studies in the Novel*, vol.29, 1997, available online.

40. Unsigned review in *The Guardian*, 2 May 1919.

41. Screenplay for *The Moon and Sixpence*, 1943.

42. Robert Hughes, *Time*, 22 March 1971.

43. W. Somerset Maugham, *The Moon and Sixpence*, London 1919, reprinted 1999, p.3.

Plate Section Introductions

Identity and Self-Mythology pp.70–91

1. Contrary to the findings of the catalogue raisonné authors (Wildenstein 2001, cat.23), I agree with the curators of the Fogg Art Museum that this is a self-portrait.

2. Conventionally posed, this photograph, by a firm of Danish photographers possibly related to Mette and proud of their Paris accreditation, 'Julie Laurberg and Gad', shows Mette seated and Gauguin in debonair pose behind her, leaning on a couple of weighty tomes. Repr. Wildenstein 2001, p.596.

3. According to Druick and Zegers et al., exh.cat. *Van Gogh and Gauguin: The Studio of the South*, The Art Institute of Chicago and the Van Gogh Museum, Chicago, IL, 2001, pp.362–3.

4. See Druick and Zegers, idem, pp.257–68, and P. Dagen, 'Têtes coupées, Gauguin lecteur de Villiers de l'Isle-Adam', in *Gauguin, actes du colloque*, La Documentation française, Paris 1991, pp.213–25.

5. Letter from Gauguin to Émile Bernard, datable to November/December 1889, Malingue 1946, CVI, pp.192–4 (misdated June 1890).

6 The *Self-Portrait as Severed Head* appears as a receptacle for flowers in *Still Life with Japanese Print*, 1889, Teheran Museum of Art.

7. Letter 817 from Gauguin to Vincent van Gogh, 10–13 November 1889, vangoghletters.org.

8. 'Soyez amoureuses et vous serez heureuses' is difficult to render in English: 'Be in love and you will be happy' or just 'Love and be happy' perhaps.

9. Both Gauguin's Impressionist mentors, Pissarro and Degas, remarked upon his inveterate appropriation of exotic sources, Pissarro less sympathetically than Degas.

10. Meijer de Haan's large painting *Uriel Dacosta*, now lost, which he exhibited in 1888, dealt with the tragic story of a seventeenth-century Jewish convert to Catholicism who had reverted to Judaism, events that led to his excommunication and eventual suicide. See exh.cat. *Meijer de Haan: le maître caché*, Amsterdam and Paris 2010, pp.26–31.

11. De Haan, according to a later witness, had brought a collection of reproductions of Quattrocento Italian art to Pont-Aven. Cf. Caroline Boyle-Turner in op. cit., p.89.

12. June Hargrove, in her article 'Gauguin's Maverick Sage', explores these various questions in depth, *Van Gogh Studies 3*, pp.87–111.

13. I am grateful to Jodi Hauptmann for communicating Arnaud Toussaint's discovery of the origin of this text. The transcribed passage dealing with prostitution in London comes from chapter VIII, pp.111–12.

14. This fragile little painting was the focus of a whole exhibition, 'Gauguin's "Nirvana", Painters at Le Pouldu, 1889–1890', Wadsworth Atheneum, Hartford, CT, 2001, and continues to fascinate art historians.

15. The name Hardy (a possible misspelling of Henry) is the first to appear on the provenance of *Nirvana*, a work one would expect de Haan to have kept himself.

16. De Haan's letter, dated 13 December 1889, is cited in full in exh.cat. *Meijer de Haan*, Amsterdam and Paris 2010, pp.136–7. In Gauguin's letters to Émile Bernard of July and September 1890, de Haan is included in their plans to go to Tahiti. See Malingue 1946, letters CVII and CXII, pp.196, 202.

17. Letter to Mette datable to January or February 1893, CXXXV, Malingue 1946, p.240.

18. Wildenstein 1964, cat.594.

Making the Familiar Strange
pp.92–109

1. See Richard R. Brettell and Anne-Birgitte Fonsmark, exh.cat. *Gauguin and Impressionism*, Kimbell Art Museum, Fort Worth, TX, and Ordrupgaard, Copenhagen 2005, cat.43, pp.244–6. Fonsmark states that Gauguin carved the whole box from a block of wood from start to finish.

2. The importance of the ceramics for Gauguin's development of a synthetist style was conclusively shown by Merete Bodelsen's pioneering publications in the 1960s.

3. See Barbara Braun, 'Gauguin's Indian Identity: How Ancient Peruvian Pottery Inspired his Art', *Art History*, vol.9, no.1 (March 1986), pp.36–54.

4. Arosa's wide-ranging ceramic collection was featured in Auguste Demmin's authoritative *Guide de l'amateur des faiences et porcelaines*, Paris 1875, a work that ran into several editions. Among its pages were illustrations of a number of pre-Columbian examples.

5. Gauguin mischievously anticipates political conversations in the Köhlers' company in his letter to Émile Schuffenecker of 24 December 1888, in Merlhès 1989, p.243.

6. 'Il est extraordinaire qu'on puisse mettre tant de mystère dans tant d'éclat.' Mallarmé's phrase was reported by Gauguin (among other occasions) in a letter to André Fontainas, March 1899, in Malingue 1946, CLXX, p.288.

Landscape and Rural Narrative
pp.110–31

1. 'Vous êtes parisianiste. Et à moi la campagne. J'aime la Bretagne: j'y trouve le sauvage le primitif. Quand mes sabots résonnent sur ce sol de granit j'entends le ton sourd mat et puissant que je cherche en peinture. Tout celà est bien triste dirait le marsouin, mais à chaque peintre son caractère.' Letter of February 1888 from Gauguin to Émile Schuffenecker, in Merlhès 1989, p.63.

2. 'Je cherche à mettre dans ces figures désolées, le sauvage que j'y vois et qui est en moi aussi . . . Que diable, je veux aussi consulter la nature mais je ne veux pas en retirer ce que j'y vois et ce qui vient à ma pensée.' Letter 828 from Gauguin to Vincent van Gogh, on or about 13 December 1889, vangoghletters.org. Author's translation, which differs slightly from the version in the online publication of the letters.

3. See the detailed entry on this painting in Wildenstein 2001, cat.319, pp.524–9.

4. In his article 'Gauguin's Tahitian Titles', *The Burlington Magazine*, vol.109, no.769 (April 1967), pp.228–33, Bengt Danielsson revealed the limitations to Gauguin's understanding of Tahitian and the frequent non sequiturs in his resulting titles.

5. I am grateful to Richard Berrong for directing me to this highly pertinent 'missing chapter' from *Madame Chrysanthème*, published in *Le Figaro*, *Supplément littéraire*, on 7 April 1888. As well as the excursion into the mountains, Loti describes a similar swimming scene to the one found in *Noa Noa*.

Sacred Themes pp.132–49

1. This work, drafted in 1896–8, remained unpublished during Gauguin's lifetime. For Elizabeth Childs's lucid analysis, see exh.cat. *Gauguin in Tahiti*, Museum of Fine Arts, Boston 2004, pp.223–41.

2. Gauguin's Catholicism is central to Debora Silverman's study, *Van Gogh and Gauguin: The Search for Sacred Art*, New York 2000. But the contrast she establishes between the Dutch and French artists on the basis of their different religious heritages is questioned by Othon Printz, who explores the surprisingly frequent brushes Gauguin had with the reformed religion. Printz, *Gauguin et le protestantisme*, Liban 2008.

3. See Thomson 2005, pp.69–70.

4. This phrase is used by Douglas W. Druick and Peter Kort Zegers in *Paul Gauguin: Pages from the Pacific*, Auckland City Art Gallery, 1995, p.17.

5. Letter from Gauguin to Émile Bernard, summer 1890, in Malingue 1946, P.CIX.

6. Phrases taken from Gauguin's letters to the Directeur des Beaux Arts, dated 15 March 1891 and 12 June 1892 respectively, applying for and referring to his ongoing artistic mission. Archives Nationales, F21 2286, pièce 20, pièce 7.

7. This, interestingly, is how Gauguin retrospectively characterised his mission in a letter of 1903 to M. Pietri, judge in Papeete. See sale catalogue, Archives Joly-Segalen, Vente Drouot, 12 June 1992, cat. no.79. Gauguin was appealing against a punitive sentence (three months in prison and a fine of 1,000 francs) imposed for inciting his Marquesan neighbours to ignore the local gendarmerie's fines for possession of alcohol.

8. René Huyghe, ed., *Ancien culte mahorie*, 1951, repr. 2001, p.20.

9. Unpublished and incomplete letter to Mette Gauguin, datable to early 1892. Private Collection (see no.74).

10. In keeping with the vogue for literary exoticism and 'récits de voyage', a growing number of French ethnographic collections had Oceanic artefacts on display by the 1880s. One could study carved Marquesan earplugs, oar handles, a royal stool formerly belonging to the Tahitian royal family, in public collections in Paris, Boulogne and Rouen.

11. The role of the Catholic Belgian-born Moerenhout in challenging the hegemony of Protestantism in Tahiti was key. Following the publication of his authoritative book he encouraged the introduction of Catholic missions, which in turn paved the way for France's establishing a protectorate over, and then annexing, Tahiti. In his journalism which served the Catholic cause, Gauguin was essentially following Moerenhout's lead.

12. Gauguin was clearly interested in the ideas of Gerald Massey, author of various publications on comparative religion, among them The Natural Genesis, London 1883, a partial French translation of which came into his hands in 1896. According to Elizabeth Childs, op. cit., p.231, 'Gauguin accepted Massey's basic idea that all religions share a common truth based on myth.'

13. Letter to Schuffenecker, 30 October 1890, in Victor Merlhès, De Bretagne en Polynésie: Paul Gauguin, pages inédites, Taravao 1995, p.57.

Fictions of Femininity pp.150–75

1 See his letter to George-Daniel de Monfreid, 25 August 1902, in Joly-Ségalen, 1950, p.190. 'Les Espagnoles aux cheveux plaqués de saindoux, ça a été fait, archi-fait: c'est drôle cependant que je me les figure autrement.'

2. See fig.60, *Pont-Aven, Village Drama*, variously dated 1888 and 1894, which appears to offer a fuller, but more awkward version of this assumed back story.

3. This intriguing and plausible suggestion is made by Martin Gayford in *The Yellow House*, London 2006, pp.130–3.

4. 'Elle sait par coeur les noms de tous les dieux de l'Olympe maorie . . . comment ils ont créé le monde, comment ils aiment à être honorés.' *Noa Noa*, ch.VIII, p.129 (folio 68 recto), Louvre manuscript. Cf. facsimile produced as CD Rom, *Gauguin: écrivain*, ed. Isabelle Cahn, Réunion des Musées Nationaux, Paris 2003.

5. See Alan Moorehead, *The Fatal Impact: An Account of the Invasion of the South Pacific 1767–1840*, Harmondsworth 1966.

6. Letter from Vincent van Gogh to Theo, no.736, 17 January 1889. 'Il est physiquement plus fort que nous, ses passions aussi doivent être bien plus fortes que les nôtres. Puis il est père d'enfants puis il a sa femme et ses enfants dans le Danemark et il veut simultanément aller tout à l'autre bout du globe à la Martinique. C'est effroyable tout le vice versa de désirs et de besoins incompatibles que cela doit lui occasionner.' vangoghletters.org.

7. See Abigail Solomon-Godeau, 'Going Native', *Art in America*, July 1989, pp.119–28/161; Griselda Pollock, *Avant-Garde Gambits: Gender and the Colour of Art History*, Walter Neurath Lecture, London 1992; Nancy Mowll Mathews, *Gauguin: An Erotic Life*, New Haven, CT, and London, 2001; Chantal Spitz, 'Où en sommes nous cent ans après la question posée par Gauguin . . . ?' in *Paul Gauguin: Héritage et confrontations*, Papeete 2003.

8. In a note added to the 1901 edition of *Noa Noa*.

9. *Ancien Culte mahorie*, 1951, reprint 2001, p.11.

10. Among those whose work has helped to correct this picture are Merete Bodelsen, Nancy Mowll Mathews and Anne-Birgitt Fonsmark. See also the remarkably frank, albeit racially patronising, nature of the 1892 letter from Gauguin to his wife (no.74).

11. Félix Fénéon, *La Revue indépendante*, February 1888, quoted in Wildenstein 2001, vol.II, p.314.

12. I am grateful to Joseph Baillio for sharing his research on this fascinating, previously unknown work.

13. For a recent, more extensive discussion of this theme, see Heather Lemonedes in exh.cat. *Paul Gauguin, Paris 1889*, pp.165–9.

14. The seminal article on this theme is Henri Dorra's 'The First Eves in Gauguin's Eden', *Gazette des Beaux-Arts*, March 1953, pp.189–202.

15. *Noa Noa*, Louvre Manuscript, fol.9 verso.

16. For a more complex reading of this statuette and text, see Henri Dorra, *The Symbolism of Paul Gauguin: Erotica, Exotica and the Great Dilemmas of Humanity*, Berkeley 2007, pp.228–36.

17. June Hargrove, 'Against the Grain: The sculpture of Paul Gauguin in the context of his contemporaries', *Van Gogh Studies*, I, 2007, pp.72–111, and on *Oviri*, pp.96–102.

18. Charles Morice, *Paul Gauguin (Les Hommes d'aujourd'hui)* 1896, and Paris 1920, p.171.

Thomas Carlyle (1795–1881)
Sartor Resartus
Chapman and Hall, London 1888
Private Collection, Paris

Alphonse Daudet (1840–1897)
Tartarin de Tarascon
C. Marpon et E. Flammarion, Paris 1889
Private Collection, Paris

André Fontainas
L'ornement de la solitude
Mercure de France, Paris 1899
Private Collection, Brussels, provenance
André Fontainas collection

Jean de La Fontaine (1621–1695)
Fables illustrated by Maurice Boutet
de Monvel (1851–1913)
E. Plon, Nourrit et Cie, Paris 1888
Private Collection, Paris

Victor Hugo (1802–1885)
Les Misérables, with 200 illustrations
by Gustave Brion
Hetzel, Paris 1865
Private Collection, Paris

Stéphane Mallarmé (1842–1898)
L'Après-midi d'un Faune, illustrations
by Edouard Manet
A. Derenne, 1876
Prêt du Conseil Général de Seine-et-
Marne, Collection du Musée
départemental Stéphane Mallarmé,
Vulaines-sur-Seine

Somerset Maugham (1874–1965)
The Moon and Sixpence
William Heinemann, London 1919
Tate Library and Archive

John Milton (1608–1674)
Le Paradis perdu, translation by
Chateaubriand
Bernardin-Béchet libraire, Paris 1859
Private Collection, Paris

Charles Morice (1860–1919)
La Littérature de tout à l'heure
Perrin, Paris 1889
Bibliothèque Historique de la
Ville de Paris

Jehan Rictus (1867–1933)
«L'Hiver» in *Le Soliloque du pauvre*
Mercure de France, Paris 1897
Private Collection, Paris

Flora Tristan
Mémoires et pérégrinations d'une paria
Ladvocat, Paris 1838, Vol.1
Bibliothèque Historique de la
Ville de Paris

Flora Tristan
Promenades dans Londres
Delloye, Paris 1840
Bibliothèque Marguerite Durand,
Ville de Paris

Paul Verlaine (1844–1896)
Romances sans paroles
Léon Vanier, Paris 1891
Private Collection, Paris

Catalogues

*Catalogue for the auction of modern
pictures belonging to M. Gustave Arosa*
Hôtel Drouot, 25 February 1878
National Gallery of Art Library,
Washington, DC. David K.E. Bruce Fund

*Catalogue of the 7th Exhibition of
Independent Artists* 1882
Manuscript copy
Typo-Morris père et fils, rue Amelot,
Paris 1882–1884
Bibliothèque nationale de France, Paris

Catalogue de l'Exposition des XX 1889,
Vve Monnom, Bruxelles, 1889
Bibliothèque des Musées Royaux des
Beaux-Arts, Brussels

*Catalogue of the Exhibition of the
'Groupe impressionniste et synthétiste'
Café Volpini* 1889
Plates shown: 'Aux Roches noires' et '
Les Faneuses' by Paul Gauguin, 'Rêverie'
by Émile Bernard and an untitled plate
by Ludovic Nemo, pseudonym of
Émile Bernard
Watelet, Paris 1889
Institut national d'histoire de l'art, Paris

*Catalogue of the Paul Gauguin
Exhibition with frontispiece etching,
'Parau Hina Tefatou'*
Galeries Durand-Ruel, November 1893
Archives Durand-Ruel © Durand-
Ruel & Cie

*Catalogue of an auction sale of the
works of Paul Gauguin*
Hôtel Drouot, 18 February 1895,
with preface by August Strindberg
Institut national d'histoire de l'art, Paris

Catalogue of the 'Salon d'automne' 1906
Bibliothèque du Musée d'Orsay, Paris

Articles and Texts by Paul Gauguin

'Notes sur l'art à l'Exposition
Universelle'
Le Moderniste illustré, 4 and 13 July 1889
Bibliothèque Historique de la Ville
de Paris

'Natures mortes'
Essais d'art libre, January 1894, facsimile

'Sous deux latitudes'
Essais d'art libre, May 1894
Private Collection, Paris

'Armand Seguin'
Le Mercure de France, February 1895
Musée Maurice Denis, Saint
Germain-en-Laye

Paul Gauguin and Charles Morice
Noa Noa
La Revue blanche, 15 October and
1 November 1897
Bibliothèque du Musée d'Orsay, Paris

Critical Reviews

Octave Maus
'Sur l'exposition des XX'
La Cravache parisienne, 16 February–
2 March 1889
Musées Royaux des Beaux-Arts de
Belgique, Brussels. Archives de l'Art
contemporain en Belgique

Félix Fénéon (1861–1944)
'Autre groupe impressionniste'
La Cravache parisienne, 6 July 1889,
facsimile

Octave Mirbeau (1848-1917)
'Paul Gauguin'
Le Figaro, 18 February 1891, facsimile

Albert Aurier (1865–1892)
'Le Symbolisme en peinture –
Paul Gauguin'
Le Mercure de France, March 1891
Musée Maurice Denis, Saint-
Germain-en-Laye

Henri Foulquier
'L'Avenir symboliste'
Le Figaro, 24 May 1891, facsimile

Armand Seguin (1869-1904)
'Paul Gauguin'
Union Agricole et Maritime, 11 October
1891, facsimile

Albert Aurier (1865–1892)
'Le Symbolisme'
Revue Encyclopédique, 1 April 1892
Private Collection, Paris

Gustave Geffroy (1855–1926)
'Paul Gauguin'
La Justice, 12 November 1893, facsimile

Octave Mirbeau
'Retour de Tahiti'
Echo de Paris, 14 November 1893,
facsimile

Olivier Merson
'Chronique des Beaux-Arts'
Le Monde illustré, 16 December, 1893
Private Collection, Paris

Armand Dayot
'La Vie artistique, revue des expositions'
Le Figaro illustré, January 1894
Private Collection, Paris

Achille Delaroche
['From an aesthetic point of view,
concerning the painter Paul Gauguin']
'D'un point de vue esthétique, à propos
du peintre Paul Gauguin'
L'Ermitage, January 1894
Bibliothèque littéraire Jacques
Doucet, Paris

Interview with E. Tardieu
Echo de Paris, 13 May 1895, facsimile

Charles Morice
'Paul Gauguin' with portrait, illustration
by Émile Schuffenecker
Les Hommes d'aujourd'hui no.440, 1896
Private Collection

André Fontainas
'Paul Gauguin'
Le Mercure de France, January 1899
Musée Maurice Denis, Saint-
Germain-en-Laye

Victor Segalen
['Paul Gauguin in his final setting']
'Paul Gauguin dans son dernier décor'
Le Mercure de France, June 1904
Musée Maurice Denis, Saint-
Germain-en-Laye

Charles Morice
Paul Gauguin
Floury, Paris 1920
Bibliothèque du Musée d'Orsay, Paris

Miscellaneous Documents

*Invitation to the opening of the Exposition
des Artistes Impressionnistes et Synthétistes*
Café Volpini, June 16, 1889
Musée Maurice Denis, Saint-
Germain-en-Laye

*Advertisement for Le Grand Café,
boulevard des Capucines, managed
by M. Volpini*
La Revue de l'Exposition, 1889
Musée Maurice Denis, Saint-
Germain-en-Laye

Paris-Salon 1889
Paris, Hachette, 1889
Paris, Private Collection

Moorish Bath
Charles-Louis Courtry after a
painting by J.L.Gérôme 1874,
Etching 23.8 x 18.7
Musée Goupil, Bordeaux

For sale
Photograph of a painting by J.L.
Gérôme by Goupil & Co, 1873
Albumen silver print 34.3 x 26
Musée Goupil, Bordeaux

Posters

Anon
Agrandissement du *Petit Journal*,
25ème année, le mieux informé de tous
les journaux 1888
Poster, colour lithograph 187 x 132
Bibliothèque Forney, Ville de Paris

Anon
La Science illustrée, journal
hebdomadaire, 1890
Poster, colour lithograph, 52 x 36
Bibliothèque Forney, Ville de Paris

Hugo d'Alesi (1849–1906)
Chemins de fer PLM Algérie
Poster, colour lithograph 107 x 76
Bibliothèque Forney, Ville de Paris

Gustave Fraipont (1849–1923)
*Chemins de fer de l'Ouest, Normandie-
Bretagne* c.1895
Poster, colour lithograph 106 x 75
Bibliothèque Forney, Ville de Paris

Louis Bombled (1862–1927)
Journal des Voyages, lisez 'Fiancée Mexicaine', grand roman d'aventure par Louis Boussenard
Poster, colour lithograph 150 x 106
Bibliothèque Forney, Ville de Paris

Hugo d'Alési (1849–1906)
Exposition Universelle de 1900. Le Maréorama 1900
Poster, colour lithograph 198 x 130
Bibliothèque Forney, Ville de Paris

Georges Meunier (1869–1934)
Chemin de fer d'Orléans, Pont-Aven 1914
Poster, colour lithograph 103 x 74
Bibliothèque Forney, Ville de Paris

Henri Audoux
Compagnie des Messageries Maritimes, Grèce, Turquie, Mer noire… Australie, Nouvelle –Calédonie, Nouvelles-Hébrides 1889
Poster, colour lithograph 73 x 105.5
Collection of the French-Lines Association, Le Havre

David Dellepiane (1866–1932)
Cie des Messageries Maritimes, Paquebots Poste français, Australie, Indo-Chine, Océan Indien, Méditerranée, Brésil et Plata 1910
Poster, colour lithograph 104 x 74
Collection of the French-Lines Association, Le Havre

Photographs in Brittany and Martinique

Brittany
Anon
Pont-Aven, watermills and houses
Digital print from a glass negative
Musée des Civilisations de l'Europe et de la Méditerranée, Paris

Anon
Young girl in traditional costume
Digital print from a glass negative
Musée des Civilisations de l'Europe et de la Méditerranée, Paris

Anon
Young women in traditional costume
Digital print from a glass negative
Musée des Civilisations de l'Europe et de la Méditerranée, Paris

Anon
Elderly Breton couple c.1880
Photograph, albumen paper 10.5 x 6.4
Gérard Levy Collection, Paris

Anon
Local costumes from the Quimperlé region c.1880
Photograph, albumen paper 10.8 x 6.5
Gérard Levy Collection, Paris

Anon
'Quimper', young Breton couple c.1880
Photograph, albumen paper 10.3 x 6.5
Gérard Levy Collection, Paris

Noël le Boyer (1863–1967)
Pont-Aven, view of the town
Digital print from a glass negative
Médiathèque de l'Architecture et du Patrimoine, Paris

Noël le Boyer
Pont-Aven, Le bois d'amour
Digital print from a glass negative
Médiathèque de l'Architecture et du Patrimoine, Paris

Société d'excursions des amateurs de photographies
'Brittany' diorama from the French room in the Trocadéro ethnographic museum c.1895
Printed on baryta coated paper, 11.9 x 17.6
Musée du Quai Branly, Paris

Martinique
Gaston Fabre (1827– after 1900)
La Baie de St Pierre c.1875
Photograph, albumen print 20.8 x 28
Serge Kakou Collection, Paris

Gaston Fabre
[Female coal heaver], Charbonnière, Fort de France c.1875
Photograph, albumen print 26.3 x 19.4
Serge Kakou Collection, Paris

Gaston Fabre
Martinique vegetation
Digital print from a glass positive
Bibliothèque nationale de France, fonds de la société de Géographie, Paris

Firmin André Salles (1860–1929)
On the road near Fort-de-France 1899
Digital print from a glass positive
Bibliothèque nationale de France, fonds de la société de Géographie, Paris

Firmin André Salles
Washerwomen, Saint-Pierre 1899
Digital print from a glass positive, reproduced by Radiguet et Massiot
Bibliothèque nationale de France, fonds de la société de Géographie, Paris

Prints
The Calvary of Sainte-Anne d'Auray in Brittany 1852
Handblocked wood engraving
49.3 x 37.5
Musée départemental breton, Quimper

Notre-Dame de Rumengol, Patron saint of Brittany 1858
Handbocked wood engraving
35.5 x 24
Musée départemental breton, Quimper

Frédéric Sorrieu (1807–?)
Souvenir of Lower Brittany
Album of 15 engravings c.1860
Musée départemental breton, Quimper

Books
Henry Blackburn (1830–1897) and Randolph Caldecott (1846–1886)
Breton Folk: An Artistic Tour in Brittany
Sampson Low, Marston, Searle & Rivington, London, 1883
Private Collection, Paris

Alfred de Courcy
'Le Breton' from the series *Les Français peints par eux-mêmes*
J. Philippart, Paris 1876
Private Collection, Paris

Gustave Flaubert (1821–1880)
Par les champs et par les grèves, voyage en Bretagne
G. Charpentier et Cie, Paris 1886
Private Collection, Paris

Alphonse Joanne (1813–1881)
Guide du Finistère
Hachette, Paris, 1900
Private Collection, Paris

Pierre Loti
Mon frère Yves
Calmann Lévy, Paris 1892
Private Collection, Paris

André Petitcolin (1865–1920)
Arvor
E. Plon, Nourrit et Cie, Paris 1898
Private Collection, Paris

Magazines
['All Saints' Day in Brittany, morning service] 'La Toussaint en Bretagne, l'Office du matin'
L'Illustration, 3November 1892
Private Collection, Paris

'A girl of Pont-Aven'
The London Illustrated News, Saturday, 30 December 1876
Private Collection, Paris

Caumery (Maurice Languereau, known as, 1867–1941) and Joseph Pinchon (1871–1953)
[The childhood of Bécassine: 'Bécassine does some cooking', 'Bécassine starts school'] L'Enfance de Bécassine: 'Bécassine fait la cuisine', 'Bécassine commence ses études'.
La semaine de Suzette, no.13 and 17, 1 and 29 May 1913
Private Collection, Paris

Postcards
Pont-Aven, general view
Pont-Aven, the old road to Concarneau
Pont-Aven, the bridge and the road to Concarneau
Pont-Aven, boulders in the stream of the Aven
Pont-Aven, little girl going to market
Le Pouldu, Hôtel des Grands sables
Musée de Pont-Aven

Pont-Aven, view of the harbour looking downstream
Pont-Aven, entrance to the Bois d'amour
Pont-Aven, the Trémalo chapeLe Pouldu, Porz-Guen
Le Pouldu, general view of the Grands sables
Environs of Pont-Aven, the Nizon calvary
Private Collection, Paris

The Universal Exhibition of 1889

Photographs
Anon
Palais des Machines, façade
Photograph (contretype)
Bibliothèque Historique de la Ville de Paris / Roger-Viollet

Anon
Palais des Machines and École Militaire
Photograph (contretype)
Bibliothèque Historique de la Ville de Paris / Roger-Viollet

Anon
['General history of domestic architecture'] 'Histoire générale de l'Habitation, view of a street'
Photograph (contretype)
Bibliothèque Historique de la Ville de Paris / Roger-Viollet

Anon
[Centennial exhibition of the Fine Arts] *Exposition centennale des Beaux-Arts*
Photograph (contretype)
Bibliothèque Historique de la Ville de Paris / Roger-Viollet

Anon
Palais des colonies
Photograph (contretype)
Bibliothèque Historique de la Ville de Paris / Roger-Viollet

Anon
Javanese Dancers
Photograph mounted on card 19.6 x 24.5
Gérard Levy Collection, Paris

Neurdein Frères – Neurdein, Etienne (1832–1918), Neurdein, Louis Antonin (1846–after 1915)
View of the Javanese village and Angkor Pagoda at the Esplanade des Invalides
Photograph mounted on card, from the album 'Exposition Universelle, 1889'
13 x 18
Gérard Levy Collection, Paris

Magazines
'Etat actuel de la Tour Eiffel'
Le Monde illustré, 10 November 1888
Private Collection, Paris

'Palais des Beaux-Arts'
Le Monde illustré, 3 March 1889
Private Collection, Paris

'Petites danseuses javanaises'
Journal illustré, 23 June 1889
Private Collection, Paris

['Life in the American wild west, equestrian exercises performed by Buffalo Bill's troop'] 'La vie sauvage dans l'ouest américain, exercices équestres de la troupe de Buffalo Bill'
Journal des Voyages, 2 October 1889
Private Collection, Paris

['Official award ceremony'] 'Distribution solennelle des récompenses'
Le Monde illustré, 6 October 1889
Private Collection, Paris

['The central gallery of the Palais des Machines, on the evening of the Exhibition's closure'] 'La Galerie centrale du Palais des Machines le soir de la clôture de l'Exposition'
Le Monde illustré, 10 November 1889
Private Collection, Paris

Ethnographic Museums
Photographs
Société d'excursions des amateurs
de photographie
*Paris Ethnographic Museum, the
American room* c.1895
Photograph mounted on card 17 x 12
Musée du Quai Branly, Paris

Société d'excursions des amateurs
de photographie
*Paris Ethnographic Museum, Oceanian
objects and casts of Indochinese carvings*
c.1895
Photograph mounted on card 17.6 x 24
Musée du Quai Branly, Paris

Société d'excursions des amateurs
de photographie
*Paris Ethnographic Museum,
Oceanian objects and casts of Indochinese
carvings* c.1895
Photograph mounted on card 11.5 x 16
Musée du Quai Branly, Paris

Anon
Paris Ethnographic Museum c.1890–9
*Life-size models of indigenous people
from the Solomon Islands – San Cristolval,
Hawaii – Samoan woman printing
bark cloth*
Photographs mounted on card
8.9 x 8.9, 8.5 x 8.9, 9 x 8,9
Musée du Quai Branly, Paris

Anon
*The Auckland Museum in Princes
Street* c.1890
Digital print from a glass plate negative
Auckland Museum, Auckland

Magazines
'The Ethnographic Museum at
the Trocadéro'
La Nature, 1892
Private Collection, Paris

'Kanak Chief at the Ethnographic
Exhibition'
Le Monde illustré, 14 décembre 1878
Private Collection, Paris

Oceania

Photographs
Jules Agostini (1859–1930)
*Gauguin's house and studio in Punaauia,
Tahiti* 1897
Digital print from a glass negative
Musée du Quai Branly, Paris

Susan Hoare
Group of Tahitian women c.1885
Photograph, albumen print 19.8 x 15.8
Serge Kakou Collection, Paris

Susan Hoare
*Evite, Atupa and Naehu, Tahitian
dancers* c.1880–9
Photograph, albumen paper 12.9 x 9.8
Musée du Quai Branly, Paris

Attributed to Frank Holmes
*House of the Governor, Papeete,
Tahiti* c.1900
Photograph, aristotype print 11.7 x 16.8
Serge Kakou Collection, Paris

Henri Lemasson (1870–1956)
*'Where do we Come From? What are
we? Where are we Going?' in Gauguin's
studio* 2 June 1898
Photograph, albumen print 13 x 18
Centre des Archives d'Outre-Mer,
Aix-en-Provence

Attributed to Henri Lemasson
Tahitian woman 1897
Photograph, silver print 16.9 x 11.9
Serge Kakou Collection, Paris

Henri Lemasson
The road at Punaauia, Tahiti c.1896
Digital print from a glass negative
Centre des Archives d'Outre-Mer,
Aix-en-Provence

Henri Lemasson
View of Atuona, Marquesas Islands c.1896
Digital print from a glass negative
Centre des Archives d'Outre-Mer,
Aix-en-Provence

Henri Lemasson
*The Church in Atuona, Marquesas
Islands* c.1896
Digital print from a glass negative
Centre des Archives d'Outre-Mer,
Aix-en-Provence

Henri Lemasson
Atiheu Bay, Marquesas Islands c.1897
Photograph, gelatin-silver print
13.2 x 17.9
Serge Kakou Collection, Paris

Charles Georges Spitz (1857–1894)
*Street in the 'Petite Pologne' quarter
of Papeete, Tahiti* c.1890
Photograph, aristotype print by
Frank Holmes 17.4 x 23
Serge Kakou Collection, Paris

Charles Georges Spitz
Fishing scene near Afaahiti, Tahiti c.1890
Photograph, aristotype print by Frank
Holmes 16.5 x 21.7
Serge Kakou Collection, Paris

Charles Georges Spitz
Tahitian village c.1890
Photograph, aristotype print by Frank
Holmes 18.4 x 22.7
Serge Kakou Collection, Paris

Charles Georges Spitz
Fruit pickers c.1890
Photograph, aristotype print by Frank
Holmes 21.7 x 16.5
Serge Kakou Collection, Paris

Charles Georges Spitz
Fountain in the rock, Samoan Islands
c.1888
Photograph, aristotype print by Frank
Holmes 22.9 x 17
Serge Kakou Collection, Paris

George D. Valentine
The Wharf, Papeete, Tahiti 1887
Photograph, albumen print 18.9 x 29.1
Serge Kakou Collection, Paris

Documents
**Photographs and reproductions
of artworks**
Anon
Photo of a Tahura Tablette
Photograph, print on silver paper
from a glass negative 8.6 x 12.6
Private Collection, Paris

Gustave Arosa Studio
*Plate from the Parthenon Frieze,
Man with a horse* 1868
Collotype 19.5 x 23.5
Jean-Yves Tréhin Collection, Paris

Gustave Arosa Studio
Plate from the Parthenon Frieze,
Group of horsemen 1868
Collotype 23.5 x 31.5
Jean-Yves Tréhin Collection, Paris

Gustave Arosa Studio
*Plate from the Panathenean Frieze,
Four standing figures* 1868
Collotype 23.5 x 22.5
Jean-Yves Tréhin Collection, Paris

Photographs
Anon
Erotic photograph, Port-Saïd c.1890
Albumen print 27.1 x 20.3
Gérard Lévy Collection, Paris

Anon
Erotic photograph, Port-Saïd c.1890
Albumen print 26.3 x 20
Gérard Lévy Collection, Paris

Le Sourire
Le Sourire
Number 1, August 1899, hand-tinted
with watercolour by Gauguin
Musée des Beaux-Arts, Chartres

Le Sourire
Number 2, September 1899
Musée des Beaux-Arts, Chartres

'La vie d'un géomètre', 'Gallet-
Rousselle est bon enfant'
Songs by Paul Gauguin
Papeete, 1900
Musée des Beaux-Arts, Chartres

Magazines
'Les Anthropophages'
Journal des Voyages, 2 June 1878
Private Collection, Paris

A. Pailhès
'Souvenirs du Pacifique, Archipel
de Tahiti'
Le Tour du Monde, 1876
Private Collection, Paris

Annexion de Tahiti à la France
L'illustration, 18 September 1880
Private Collection, Paris

Pierre Loti
'Un chapitre inédit de *Madame
Chrisanthème*'
Le Figaro supplément littéraire,
7 April 1888
Private Collection, Paris

Pierre de Myrica
'Tahiti'
Le Tour du Monde, 1902
Private Collection, Paris

Books
Louis Henrique (1848–1906)
*Les colonies françaises, vol.IV, Colonies
et protectorats de l'Océan pacifique*
Maison Quantin, Paris 1889
Private Collection, Paris

Pierre Loti
Rarahu: Le mariage de Loti
Calmann Lévy, Paris 1888
Private Collection, Paris

Jacques Antoine Moerenhout
(1796––1879)
Voyages aux Iles du grand Océan,
two volumes
Arthur Bertrand, Paris 1837
Bibliothèque Historique de la Ville
de Paris

*Te Faufaa Api, a to tatou fatu e te ora a
iesu Mesia ra: iritihia ei parau Tahiti; ...*
The New Testament, translated into
Tahitian by Henry Nott, London 1853
Edinburgh University Library

*Exposé des faits qui ont accompagné
l'agression des français contre l'Ile de
Tahiti ...*
[Brief statement of the aggression of
the French on the Island of Tahiti ...]
translated into French by the London
Missionary Society
L.–R. Delay, Paris 1843
Edinburgh University, New College
Library

Postcards
*Marseille, Embarcation of the Messageries
maritimes
The Australien
The Armand Béhic
View of Moorea
Papenoo valley
Papeete
Papeete, quai du commerce
Moorea, house of a publicworker
Tahitian woman
Tattooed Marquesan
Tepairu
Old woman reading the Bible*
Private collection, Paris

LENDERS AND CREDITS

INDEX